ianzen Jeanne Allen Julia Allen Joe Al

Dan Arons Christine Arthur Lisa Arve

fer Baker Marwan Bakri Jennifer Balderson Megan Baratka

isa Barton Michele Beauchine Chloe Beirne Brian Benenato

eff Bolen Robyn Boxie **Rebecca Boylan** Thalia Bremis

n Tara Brown Thom Brown Jennifer Buck Cleary Buckley

ch Richards Michael Bush Frank Caliri Jonathan Campbell

Carvajal Jeffrey Causey Betsy Chabot Elizabeth Chang

Chase Johnny Chern Carol Chiles Ryan Christenberry

Cohen Linda Cohen Jackie Collins-Hughes Lauren Compton

per Sarah Cordner Jason Costello **Matt Cotton**

eather Crook Ryan Crosslin Scott Culley Christine Curran

De Almeida Aimee DeCicco David DeFilippo Christi DeLarco

a Dowaliby Elizabeth Dressler Francis Durkin Trish Duval

d El-Khoury Betsy Ellor Irene Elsinovsky **Steve Enright**

ner Aaron Famosi Patricia Fantuzzi Welbourn Jennifer Fekete

Folz Patricia Fong Bill Foucher Eric Foulke **Chu Foxlin**

ong Jeanne Gachoya Christie Gamp Valeri Gage Jill Garzik

aria Goddard-Vidal Chris Goldthwaite Justin Gologorsky

Madhu Gresla Gabriella Gross-Bogran Caroline Guerrero Perez

en Tammy Hafen Herb Hale Mark Hall Julie Hammers

Harrison Andrew Hazelton Erin Heath Marylin Hernandez

than Huang Jane Hughes **Alec Iacono** Glenn Inghram

ustin Jennings Shikha Jindal Debra Johnson Paul Joyce

an Suzanne Kenney Kevin Kiley Minna Kim Sangmoo Kim

thy Knight **Rick Kobus** Nicholas Koulbanis Teresa Krue

k Carolyn Langan Cynthia LaRue Kimberly Law Phil Lee

ncy Linné Megan Littlejohn Tracy Long Zobeida Lopez Osorio

TSOI / KOBUS & ASSOCIATES

Published in Australia in 2008 by
The Images Publishing Group Pty Ltd
ABN 89 059 734 431
6 Bastow Place, Mulgrave, Victoria 3170, Australia
Tel: +61 3 9561 5544 Fax: +61 3 9561 4860
books@imagespublishing.com
www.imagespublishing.com

The Images Publishing Group Reference Number: 798

National Library of Australia Cataloguing-in-Publication entry:

Title:	Tsoi/Kobus & Associates.
ISBN:	9781864702842 (hbk.)
Notes:	Includes index.
Subjects:	Tsoi/Kobus & Associates.
	Architectural firms – United States – Massachusetts.
	Architecture, American.
Also Titled:	Tsoi/Kobus and Associates.
Dewey Number:	720.9744

Coordinating editor: Andrew Hall

Designed by The Graphic Image Studio Pty Ltd, Mulgrave, Australia
www.tgis.com.au

Digital production by Splitting Image Colour Studio Pty Ltd, Australia
Printed by Everbest Printing Co. Ltd., in Hong Kong/China

THE MASTER ARCHITECT SERIES

TSOI / KOBUS & ASSOCIATES

ARCHITECTURE • PLANNING • INTERIOR DESIGN

images
Publishing

Contents

General Practice

Planning

On the Boards

Timeline and Credits

Vision and Philosophy

Tsoi/Kobus & Associates was founded on a belief in the power of technology and the promise it holds for building types of all kinds. From the early days of our practice, we have sought to apply rigor and beauty in equal measure to the design of even the most technologically complex projects. This principle has guided our search for design solutions that accommodate intensive technical demands while demonstrating sensitivity to human needs for comfort, dignity, and inspiration.

As architects, planners, and interior designers, we believe that our primary role is to lead our clients to solutions that not only address their building needs but also advance their strategic goals. Our philosophy manifests itself in a design approach that is both innovative and practical, that is rooted in our clients' missions, that relies on intensive collaboration, and that ends with smart architecture rather than celebrating smart architects. We create spaces that support the delivery of compassionate healthcare, that accelerate discovery, that promote learning, and that enhance the quality of human interaction.

Our clients share our technological imperative and our commitment to ambitious and humane goals. Working with them as allies, we approach each project not only as an opportunity for memorable design but also as an opportunity to improve our clients' performance and enrich the lives of their constituents. Our best results come from a thorough integration of holistic thinking, thoughtful design, and technical expertise.

In our work and in our relationships—with clients, with peers, and with each other—we strive for responsiveness, authenticity, and credibility. It is in achieving these aims that we measure our success and demonstrate our respect for both the art and the enterprise of our profession.

Introduction

Ed Tsoi (left) and Rick Kobus

A conversation with Stephen A. Kliment, FAIA

Edward T.M. Tsoi, FAIA
Richard L. Kobus, FAIA, FACHA

One of the great challenges of the 21st century lies in the tension between technology and the human environment. We can capture images of stars 17,000 light years from Earth, design and deliver a skyscraper in China without ever setting foot there, and operate an array of medical devices that can diagnose and heal illnesses in ways unheard of even two decades ago.

Architecture is in the rare position of reconciling the gap, of creating spaces that serve human needs while accommodating ever-changing technology, improving performance, advancing business goals, and boosting sustainability. Tsoi/Kobus & Associates (TK&A), the Cambridge-based architectural, planning, and interior design firm, which in 2008 celebrates its first 25 years in practice, is squarely in the center of these challenges.

This book describes how the firm realized its goals to create effective, attractive spaces that marry technology and humanity—and considers where this philosophy is expected to lead the firm in the future.

TK&A is well known among peers and clients for its planning and design of healthcare facilities of every kind—teaching, acute care, clinical care, and research. They are pioneers in incorporating new medical technology, such as proton therapy, a cancer treatment that uses proton beams to deliver a powerful dose of radiation directly to a tumor, into first-of-a kind building prototypes. The firm's portfolio also includes an array of projects that reflect the latest mechanical technology in a user-friendly setting, including college and university buildings, facilities for science and technology, marine resource centers, structures to house biomedical science, investment office buildings, even conversion of an early 20th-century automobile production plant into a home for high-tech tenants.

TK&A also has championed the latest techniques for controlled project delivery—from various design-to-build arrangements to collaborative software and technologies. But the firm isn't just embracing a trend. In the judgment of the founding partners, Edward T. M. Tsoi, FAIA and Richard L. Kobus, FAIA, FACHA, these tools are essential to providing their clients an effective, high-caliber service, from pre-design to post-occupancy.

Finally, Tsoi and Kobus see architecture not only as an art and a science but also as a business—their business and their clients'. If the design doesn't work to advance a client's business, it has failed. If TK&A's own business doesn't make a profit—fortunately, it has done so—then something in the strategic planning and delivery process needs fixing.

Tsoi and Kobus come from similar family backgrounds—Tsoi's father was an architect, Kobus' a contractor, and both have brought to the firm an upbeat, compassionate, informed outlook that has shaped the firm's culture. Initiative is encouraged, responsibility is delegated, individual careers are watched over, leadership is rewarded. The firm's Harvard Square offices are laid out and organized for tasking and teaming so teams can work together and regroup as new projects come in. As the following conversation shows, there's a can-do aura that attracts top talent to the firm and keeps it there.

—Stephen A. Kliment, FAIA, New York, March 2008

KLIMENT: What did you hope to achieve when you began Tsoi/Kobus & Associates in 1983? Have those goals changed over time?

KOBUS: Ed and I spent a number of years together in the Boston office of Skidmore, Owings and Merrill (SOM). We had the extraordinary experience there of joining a relatively modest office—more of a field office, really—and growing it into a significant architectural presence in Boston in just three or four years.

The lessons we learned from building up that office—attracting good people and seeing them flourish, with great opportunity, great clients, and great projects—served as something of a prototype for our own firm.

When we decided to go out on our own, we wanted to create a firm that offered a rich, professional environment that attracted the best people, drew the most out of them, and attracted great clients. We envisioned a firm that people would want to stay with and feel that it was where they could achieve their professional goals and ambitions. We were going to create that sort of platform and we believed that if we got it right, we could create great architecture.

TSOI: One of the things I had admired at SOM was that they provided architecture, planning, and interior design. Integrating the scales was important to them, and it became important to us. From the time we started the firm, we have believed that client input is an integral component of our process. The clients need us to advise them, but they in turn must have a voice. We have built a strong reputation on that attitude.

KOBUS: On many projects, the client is not necessarily the person who hires you. When we do a research facility, the individual scientists become our clients. The patients become our clients in the healthcare environment. Students and faculty become our clients in a teaching environment. Understanding the whole complexity of the client we're serving has changed the way we do our work.

KLIMENT: They know what they want, but they don't necessarily know what they need.

KOBUS: And they don't really know how to translate it into architecture. When we started the firm, I felt that from a business point of view, architecture was a fairly straightforward business, and we should keep it that way. We shouldn't complicate the business arrangements, and we ought to live up to our management responsibilities to our clients.

KLIMENT: In your 25 years in practice, what accomplishments do you value most, and why?

TSOI: I would measure them by the degree to which we have made our clients successful. One of our most gratifying recent experiences was developing a particular healthcare building type: proton facilities. There, our contribution was not just in the architecture, but in architecture integrating the technology, the patient experience, and the care providers in a tight, technically demanding, expensive building type, and finding the formula that optimizes the "payback" to each stakeholder.

Our concern isn't just the look and feel of the outside elevation, or even the interior features. We worry about how the buildings function over time, and how they support the mission established by our clients. There are the clients who pay us, and others who are the client's clients—the actual users—who also must be satisfied.

KOBUS: A second point I'm proud of is that we've succeeded in creating the rich professional environment we set out to. It attracts top-caliber people and keeps them. Our retention rate is very high. It affords us a high degree of intelligence and efficiency so we can work smarter. And it gives us a level of dependability with our clients that has contributed to our very high client repeat rate. We often follow clients to other destinations as they go from one organization to another. On average, year to year, about two-thirds of our business is repeat business.

Steve Kliment (center)

TSOI: Another contribution we both value has been our impact on our profession. For example, we have worked on improving the quality of contracts. Rick and I have served on the Boston Society of Architects board to help find ways to improve what we give back to society as architects.

KLIMENT: How do you select and manage your market sectors?

KOBUS: We made an early decision to stay primarily in markets that had high barriers to entry: healthcare, science and technology, and college and university. That was a conscious decision to work in areas where it was relatively difficult to compete. It also means that the fees are higher. People pay for value. You have to be a smarter firm to participate in those markets.

KLIMENT: Name some core principles that shape your firm's design philosophy.

KOBUS: Every good design starts with a clear diagram—a simplification of all the design's complexities distilled into a discernible, clear diagram—the parti, if you will. Every design decision from there on has to support that diagram. Another aspect for me is that materials have to be used honestly, intelligently, and with a lot of clarity. As a student and young architect, I was greatly influenced by the work of Louis Kahn and by Michael McKinnell and Gerhard Kallmann. We think about the craft of how materials are used. That's a really critical part of our work. And since our projects are typically technologically oriented, they have to function appropriately.

But we should not be enslaved by that understanding. You have to use it as a springboard to create architecture, not as shackles to stop you from doing architecture.

TSOI: I believe that form doesn't follow function so much as function shapes form. We seek to make form not just an expression of those functions, but a celebration of them. That gives us a license for interpretation. I agree when Rick talks about respect for materials. It's also respect for the engineering components that make up our buildings. The richness that drives both our interiors and exteriors lies in part in the art of integrating all of the systems into the building. Added to that, our buildings are largely driven by their role in the cityscape. We work on very few buildings that simply sit in the middle of nowhere. As a student at Penn, I picked up a real respect for the complexities of urban form—what drives it and how every building plays a role in either enhancing clarity and function, or working against it. With so many of our buildings, even when we're not commissioned to do the urban design background plan or the master plan of which the building is a part, we end up doing it anyway in order to inform movement, form, color, materials, texture, and accent. You always need to understand the larger context.

KLIMENT: The Center for Life Science Boston, with its glass and steel and curved form, seems a departure from your more typical design vocabulary.

KOBUS: We broke a lot of molds with that building. It was done by a private developer in the Longwood Medical Area. A district plan suggested there ought to be a 12-story building that would fit in with the adjacent 12-story buildings. We worked on the massing, but it would have created a monotonous 12-story-high, nearly 1000-foot-long wall. We started experimenting with how to break up this volume, to make it feel more vertical than it really was. We also experimented with breaking through that 12-story limit. There was a "glass ceiling" in the Longwood Medical Area: nobody had ever gone above 300 feet. But nobody had really challenged it either, so we started working with building forms that broke through that ceiling. Doing so created a unique spot in the city. When you're in the space, you don't realize the building is nearly 50 percent taller than the surrounding buildings. And you have the powerful gesture of a curving 20-story form marking the corner of Blackfan Square—a modern-day campanile of sorts.

KLIMENT: I read about an experiment where two groups of patients with dissimilar illnesses were placed in two different categories of space. One looked out of the window at a brick wall. The other saw a nice garden. Researchers found that the length of recovery of patients in the room with a view was half the time of the other. How do you respond to that?

TSOI: When you're compromised in terms of your health, it matters a lot that you have a connection with sun, light, the weather, and the rhythm of the day. When you're inside a room and can't tell when it's 10 o'clock in the morning or 10 o'clock at night, it throws your system off.

In a healthcare environment, it's even more important than in almost any other building type to maintain that rhythm.

KOBUS: Stress plays an enormous role in the healing process. The more stress a patient feels, the less rapidly the body heals. A friend of mine once said to me that a patient is a stranger in a strange land. Your control is taken away. In the process of trying to heal you, people tell you when to wake, when to sleep, when to eat, what to eat, what medications to take, what clothes to wear or not to wear. As designers, we do everything we can to reduce the stress level, make the environment more familiar, and put a sense of control back in the patient's hands.

KLIMENT: There's a lot of talk nowadays of an office culture. Do you have one, what is it, and how do you maintain it?

KOBUS: I don't take credit for creating the culture at Tsoi/Kobus & Associates. The firm has created its own culture. The common denominators are a great love of the art of architecture and a tremendous commitment to collegial, respectful, and successful relationships, both internally and externally. There's a real drive to excellence, a belief that even if we've done it well once, we can do it better the next time.

KLIMENT: Define "excellence."

KOBUS: It means a philosophy of constant improvement. I'm not sure that you ever achieve excellence, per se. But we're never satisfied that because we did it right one time that that's the solution forever. That thinking applies to our relationships and our communications. It's true about our design product and about our design process. Our people are constantly looking to improve upon what we're doing. That's very much a part of the culture of the firm. Ed and I started it, but it developed a strong internal momentum that we're very proud of.

KLIMENT: Every firm bears a lot of the personality of its founders. What about Tsoi/Kobus & Associates?

TSOI: One of our founding principles has been that architecture is a collaborative sport, that there is no one who works so brilliantly that he or she can afford to work solo. The process of bringing an idea from a seed to a built edifice you can walk through and feel proud of demands so much talent of different kinds that there's no single person in this office, or in any office that I can think of, where that talent is so sophisticated and so concentrated in one person.

There is here a sense of developing younger people. Each of us, no matter where we are in the chain—if you're not bringing someone along, you haven't risen to the whole challenge.

KLIMENT: Do you think young architects should be forgiven for occasionally making a mistake?

TSOI: Absolutely. We have groups in the office who work across all the market sectors, as well as an architects' forum, a group of younger designers who call themselves PUSH.

KOBUS: PUSH has sought to push the envelope of our design knowledge and expertise, whether it's sustainability, new materials, or a different approach. It's really fun to see them work. It's almost like an underground culture. They manage themselves, organize themselves, and have their own exercises.

Take the use of technology, for instance. They push the use of BIM. They have really gotten behind the idea of 3-D design and moved it from the simplicity of SketchUp, which is a fairly awkward tool, to a sophisticated level of discussion. For the Center for Life Science Boston, one of the members of the team did a spectacular analysis of the building in three dimensions, looking at how the parts of the building come together to express the skin, the bones, and the tissues.

TSOI: We respect the kind of natural inquisitiveness that younger architects have. We don't say, "Look, if you don't do it the way Rick likes it or Ed likes it, you're never going to get ahead." In fact, PUSH established a kind of reverse culture: if you're not pushing the envelope, you may not get invited to be the designer on the next project.

KLIMENT: Does Tsoi/Kobus & Associates have a company "style?" If somebody were to take your last 25 buildings and stand them next to each other, would there be signs of a common vocabulary?

TSOI: Somebody who really knows our work probably could pick out a TK&A building, but not your average citizen.

KOBUS: These are matters we were talking about earlier. Respect for materials, respect for the way materials are used, respect for light, respect for craft—I think those are the signatures of virtually all of our work. But I don't think that there's a singular look as there's a singular look for, say, Frank Gehry.

KLIMENT: How does the business side of your practice set you apart from other firms?

TSOI: Running an architectural firm is difficult. It's not like you manufacture 10 widgets, get paid when you sell them, and then go manufacture the next 10. You've got clients who, for the first phase, you could be beating your head against the wall and they don't like anything and you just keep doing it and doing it again. Yet there's an implied obligation that the architect ultimately meets the expectations and requirements of the client, and every client is different.

How do you make money at a business like that? We have to understand early on what the client is looking for, and how to manage the process in an economical way so that we deliver the most good for the effort that's put in, and we're also able to make a living at it. If you look at some of the design-emphasis firms, they're apt to make money on the backs of their employees. They have young people working long hours. I couldn't stand to do that to my staff. Then there are other firms that seem to think it's all about making money and delivering products, and that's almost shameful.

KOBUS: The old phrase "Design is a patient search," is absolutely true. But it's not an endless search. Too often, architects make the mistake of thinking that if you haven't tried everything, you haven't searched far enough. As you mature and gain perspective, you begin to understand that the range of opportunities that actually fit the program at hand is fairly narrow. Part of our success has been to define that range efficiently, and share it with clients so they can participate in choices and know that nothing has been left off the table.

KLIMENT: What about project budgets?

TSOI: We drive home the responsibility to watch the money. We tell clients they cannot have an infinite number of hours of staff time, so how do we budget it? We have driven financial responsibility all the way down to the team level. Our staff understands that if they get a quarter of the way through but spent half the time budget, somebody is going to be asking questions. And our office culture, if you will, respects that.

KOBUS: Managers make it clear that everybody shares responsibility for getting to the deadline or the next presentation. After the meeting, we will debrief and talk about what went well, what we need to work on more, and what the work plan is to get to the next meeting.

TSOI: Some firms argue half in jest that if you're not losing money, it must not be a great project, because design means spending inordinate amounts of time on it. But some of our best designs are right on budget. Frankly, I think our clients would rather know that we make a fair profit—if we can watch our own house, they can feel confident that we're going to be watching their dollars, too.

KLIMENT: TK&A has been in business for 25 years. Over the years you must have developed an approach to business development. Can you describe it?

KOBUS: Our marketing staff is not organized by building type. They are experts at knowing our work, how our work fits into the fields that we work in and that our competitors work in. They are not design professionals, so our senior architects contact our prospects. We don't believe that clients want to speak to salespeople; clients want to speak to the people who are going to do the work.

We gather a lot of benchmarking data and other information of great value to our clients. For example, in our academic medical center market, we have a great wealth of information about types and sizes of buildings, utilization, what buildings cost, and how many research dollars per square foot these organizations are doing. We can share that with clients as a way of helping them frame a project they're thinking about. Often we use that knowledge base as a wedge to introduce ourselves to a client and hope to serve them before we've actually formally started to do so.

TSOI: We have used different approaches to business development over the years. We've had outsiders lead the effort and we have gone long stretches with nobody doing it in a formal way.

Ed Tsoi and Rick Kobus

By and large, it means mining information long before a project gets to be an RFP. We want to work the relationships, make sure there's a project, then gradually bring the pieces together. If we're successful, maybe there's no RFP process at all, no competition.

KOBUS: I agree with Ed. It helps to have people who network well, who are savvy about the marketplace, who know the right people, who are out there collecting, digesting, and qualifying the information they're getting.

KLIMENT: Have you worked out your succession?

TSOI: Some 10 years ago, after talking with many consultants, we wrote up a transition plan. A key tenet is to separate governance from ownership and from leadership. Governance has to be very streamlined, and it has been basically Rick and me meeting weekly over breakfast. From the standpoint of ownership, we are always thinking about what this place is going to be like as we get older or when we retire. The transition is certainly a top challenge we face; it's so important that we get it right.

KOBUS: Leadership in an architectural firm means many things. We have leaders who are deeply experienced market sector specialists. Some are brilliant at leading clients; others are gifted at mentoring younger staff. We have leaders who are extraordinary managers, who are adept at managing a massive design and construction enterprise. Others are masters of detail. Still others excel at fostering a creative process that yields innovation and delight. All such skills have played their part in the success of the firm. A key goal of any transition, including ours, is finding the right balance between strategic growth and meeting clients' expanding needs.

KLIMENT: Not every architect accepts every commission. What are your criteria?

TSOI: Size of job and reputation of the client.

KOBUS: Also, is the project of a size that we can succeed at? Some projects are too small for us. Will the client support a high-quality building? Do we have the right staff for that particular project? We actively seek out relationships with clients we want to work for. We don't necessarily wait for the RFQ to come in.

KLIMENT: As you look ahead, what are the challenges facing your firm?

KOBUS: There is a declining graduation rate of architects, and not all of those graduates are choosing to practice architecture in the conventional sense. So we face a shortage of design professionals globally.

A second challenge is that technology is finally delivering on its promise to the architectural field. This will fundamentally change the relationship among the architect, contractor, and owner in terms of how buildings are actually designed, procured, and delivered. Architects have a wonderful opportunity to redefine their relationship in that triad. With BIM, we can start the database and own it. That means you have more senior people on a project much earlier. On the other hand, it also means fewer opportunities for junior architects to learn the practice, so it's up to us to create formal training programs for younger staff.

TSOI: I have a somewhat different take. I feel that the basic tenets of design and architectural practice haven't changed a lot. It's the tools that have changed enormously. Many of them have separated the visceral aspect of design from the product we deliver. The movement of design has gotten more electronic. It's more an intellectual exercise than a tactile, experiential method of creation. But I find that five times out of seven, the big firms still do it the old-fashioned way, which is with a lot of models, a lot of testing, a lot of hand drawings, a lot of conceptual diagramming not done on the computer, but by hand.

KOBUS: I want to separate the design process from the project delivery process. In the design process, sketching, building physical models, doing anything you can to viscerally understand what you're thinking, is critical. We still use tons of tracing paper around here and build lots of physical models, and we always will.

But the computer is helping us to see things more quickly. You can travel through a 3D model instead of drawing one perspective sketch of the primary view. The fact that you can communicate that to a client and share with them the experience of seeing the building actually helps us sell design concepts much more successfully than before. So I see benefits both ways.

If we can truly create an active, knowledgeable database of the building that allows for the input of the fabrication process, the shop drawing process, the changes in the field process, in the end the owner actually receives an intelligent database about his building.

KLIMENT: Your firm has a well-deserved reputation for working on healthcare facilities at all levels, from acute care to ambulatory care and everything in between. Is this reputation helpful or not helpful in going after projects outside of healthcare?

TSOI: It probably works both for us and against us. Some clients wouldn't hire an architect who has a big log of business in healthcare if they wanted a school. Others look at our website and see versatility and complexity and ask us to participate.

KOBUS: I have always chafed at the suggestion that we're hospital architects. The real challenge in doing healthcare architecture is not just functional, but also to create spaces that support the challenging and stressful human experiences that occur in a healthcare environment. And it's not just about the patients, but also about the caregivers. For them, life can be stressful, trying, and often difficult. There need to be times for both patients and staff to have respite and to reduce stress. Architecture is positioned to provide that.

KLIMENT: How do you see the future of TK&A? New market sectors? Branch offices?

TSOI: I feel we have a really well-oiled machine here. We've never been interested in selling the firm. From the start, we set a higher objective: to develop an organization that perpetuates itself. And that's a lot harder. It is something that you hope lives longer than you do. Your impact will keep going and you prefer to think you had something to do with starting it up, not simply with making a great sale.

We worked hard at selecting people we believe will be here for the long-term, who have an investment in the firm. We've thought about incentives to attract them, keep them, train them, and reward them.

If you want to make a lot of money, you can certainly find a more lucrative profession than architecture. Our best recruiting prospects share our values. It's not just making the most money; it's the satisfaction of your own creativity and the impact you have not only on a specific client, but also on people and issues that reach far beyond this one space you've designed.

KOBUS: Oddly enough, after 25 years Ed and I have very different approaches to design. We start in different places and go through a different process. But in the end it's surprising how similar the results are. No way you can detect two different bodies of work in this office. We occasionally work together, and it's energizing and challenging because our styles are different.

KLIMENT: It sounds like the basis for a good partnership.

KOBUS: There were two individuals in the firm who worked with Ed exclusively for years, and two who worked with me, and they came out very different people. We have principals who are contributors, and we have principals who are client leaders. It works in our firm. It's good to have some who have deep market sector knowledge or a passionate commitment to design—so long as the organization provides all the other talents the client needs.

Where are we going to be three years from now? Ten years from now? In large part that depends on our next generation of leaders—how they want to

Ed Tsoi, Rick Kobus, and Steve Kliment

grow themselves and where they want to take the firm. We would like to have an office somewhere out of the Boston area. But that will require someone within the firm to grow to a position of saying, "I want to go do that. I can do that."

TSOI: A branch office will probably grow out of a commission won here but far enough away and intensive enough to justify setting up shop out there. It's easy to lose money on second, third, fourth offices. A lot of firms have tried it and closed them down. We're smart enough to try and avoid some of the pitfalls.

KOBUS: Architecture is becoming a global profession and although we're not currently practicing globally, we have in the past and I think we will in the future. We are starting to develop overseas relationships to do remote collaboration on projects. We will evolve into a more globally oriented organization over the next 10 years. It will be a fundamental change.

KLIMENT: Some final comments?

TSOI: What we have here today, 25 years later, is a unique blend of our strengths and weaknesses —both Rick's and mine. That's something we are both very proud of. My ego says the biggest compliment is that the firm perpetuates itself in a form that we would recognize. For the first generation, I think we can say it is going to look pretty similar. After that, it's hard to predict. It will probably morph. New leaders will have new ideas, but I'm confident we've built a strong foundation of values that will continue to guide the firm well into the future.

KOBUS: There is a uniqueness to the way in which this firm organizes itself to do work, serve clients, create architecture—that will perpetuate itself. People here do that willingly and of their own volition, not because Ed or I tell them to. This firm has an amazing immune system. When somebody comes in and they don't fit into the process or don't work well within the process, the firm rejects them quickly. Where does that immune system come from? From everybody in the firm. It doesn't come from Ed and me.

KLIMENT: If you could start the firm again, what would you do differently?

TSOI: We can always push the design envelope. Take greater risk—in every sense— structurally, form, color.

KOBUS: I would put greater emphasis on design. We certainly emphasize it, but we did not set out from the very beginning to distinguish ourselves as a great design firm. We were busy, caught up in building the firm and getting clients and servicing them, and not dropping the ball. Twenty-five years ago, clients, by and large, didn't place the value on design that they do today.

TSOI: You can certainly improve design over time. I don't think you can change it overnight. As new principals begin to sow their oats, I think they'll continue to push Tsoi/Kobus & Associates in that direction.

Healthcare

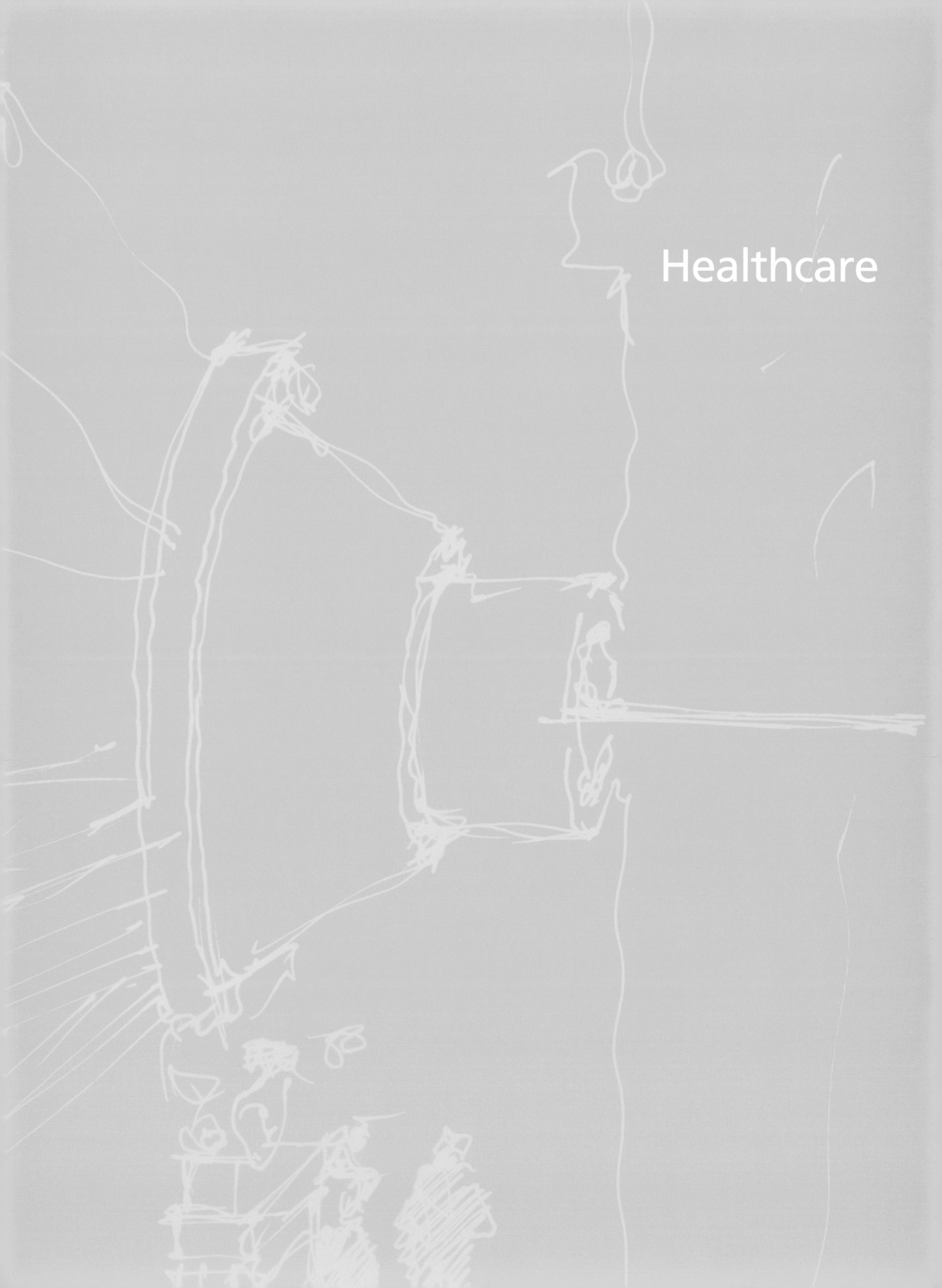

1

Location	Boston, Massachusetts
Completion	2006
Size	134,000 square feet

1 Entry detail
2 View from quadrangle

Boston Medical Center
Moakley Building

2

Streamlining access to state-of-the-art services for some of Boston's most vulnerable residents, this consolidated cancer care center reinforces Boston Medical Center's mission to provide "exceptional care without exception." Designed to support interrelated clinical, research, and teaching programs, the Moakley Building transforms the hospital campus and strengthens Boston Medical Center's relationship with its surrounding historic neighborhood. A common entry concourse links the Moakley Building to the drop-off areas and entry lobbies of Boston Medical Center's existing inpatient building and ambulatory care center, reinforcing the east–west pedestrian circulation spine that connects the hospital's two campuses and the affiliated Boston University Medical School campus.

The siting of the Moakley Building respects and enhances the open spaces that characterize the Boston Medical Center campus. A new quadrangle in the foreground helps to re-establish the formal heart of the campus and reconnects the site to the nearby Worcester Square neighborhood. An open space to the east creates a visual connection to the existing medical school quadrangle.

The building presents a gleaming glass-and-brick façade that is at once commanding and inviting. The entrance is marked by a strong four-story glass atrium that provides maximum visual connection to the outdoors and to the rest of the campus, filling the public circulation and waiting zones with soothing, diffused natural light. An open monumental stair at one end of the atrium integrates the building's levels.

Exterior materials, including brick and copper cladding, are repeated inside the facility, resulting in well-defined, human-scaled spaces that lend an air of permanence and warmth to common areas and treatment rooms. A playfully organic pattern enlivens the terrazzo floor while work by local artists brightens the interior walls.

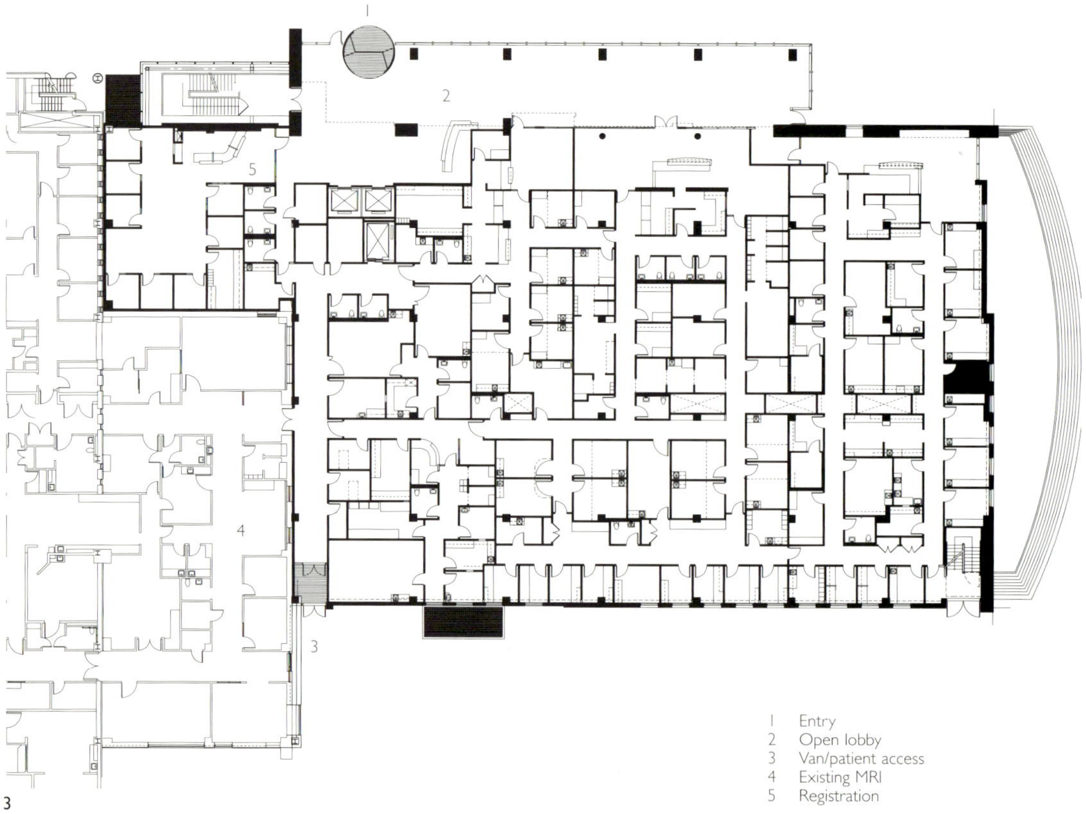

3

1 Entry
2 Open lobby
3 Van/patient access
4 Existing MRI
5 Registration

4

5

6

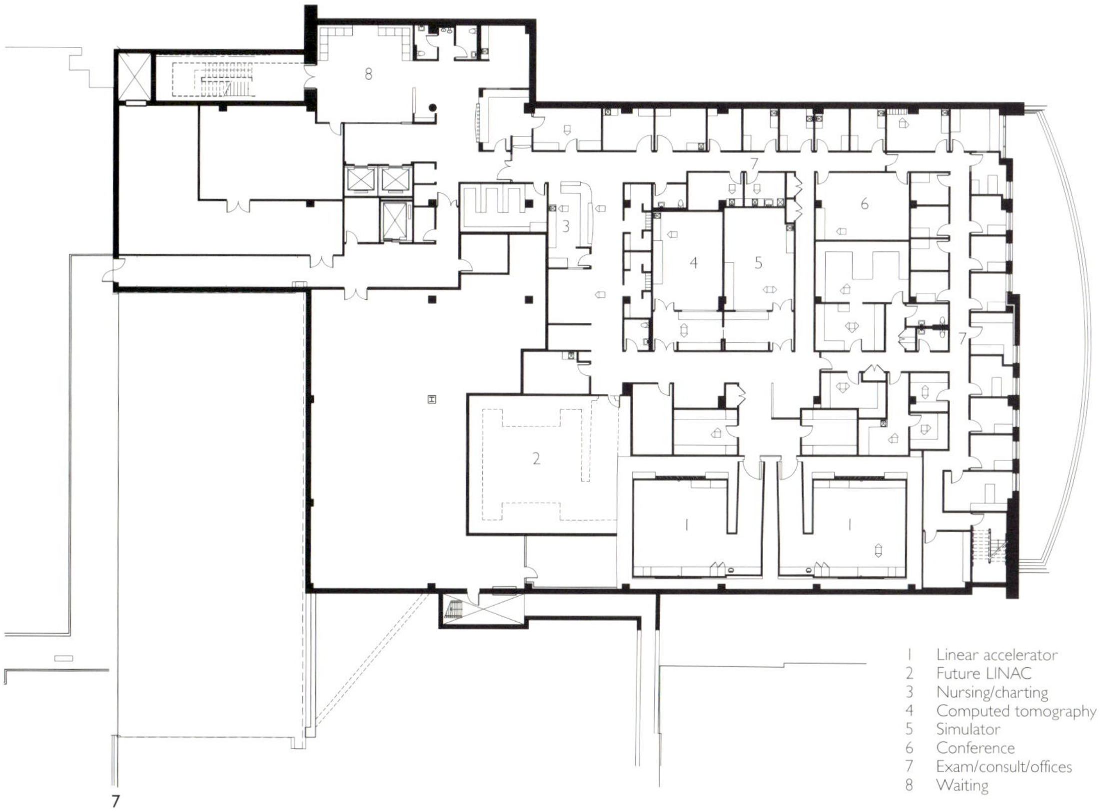

7

1 Linear accelerator
2 Future LINAC
3 Nursing/charting
4 Computed tomography (CT)
5 Simulator
6 Conference
7 Exam/consult/offices
8 Waiting

3 Entry level floor plan
4 Lobby
5 Interior detail
6 Entry detail
7 Below-grade level floor plan

Making

Location	Houston, Texas
Completion	2005 construction complete
	2006 first patient treatment
Size	84,000 square feet

The University of Texas M. D. Anderson Cancer Center

Proton Therapy Center

Opposite:
Rotunda
2 Waiting area

2

This proton therapy center is the second synchrotron-based proton facility in the United States. It provides inviting and calming spaces for the delivery of the most precise, advanced form of radiation therapy available. The two-story building contains four proton treatment rooms—three rotating gantry-style and one fixed-beam—and includes an experimental station for research, multiple smaller spaces for administrative and medical work, and patient reception and waiting areas. Essentially self-sufficient as an outpatient treatment center, the facility offers extensive space for pre-treatment evaluation, imaging, and planning.

A dramatic rotunda welcomes visitors to the entrance and references the cylindrical shape of the synchrotron contained within. The building exterior complements the aesthetic of the existing M. D. Anderson campus as well as the surrounding Southeast Texas Biotechnology Park.

The core design requirement was to accommodate the physical and technical demands of the highly sophisticated equipment associated with proton beam therapy. The proton treatment vaults, 35 feet high and capable of supporting more than 200 tons of specialized equipment, were constructed underground, using the earth as a partial radiation barrier, shored up by solid 6- to 8-foot-thick concrete roof and walls.

The building interior is organized around three primary spaces: the two-story lobby rotunda, the administrative core, and the clinical core. The lobby provides an open, light-filled common space while the administrative core presents work areas for administrators and staff, discreet non-patient visitor sections, and conference rooms. The clinical core lies at the heart of the subterranean treatment level with a layout that maximizes open space, reduces corridor lengths, and simplifies wayfinding. The atrium and a skylight deliver abundant natural light to the treatment level, creating a more pleasant environment for patients and staff.

1 Gantry
2 Treatment room
3 Clinical core
4 Corridor
5 Office
6 Patient library
7 Waiting
8 Switchyard

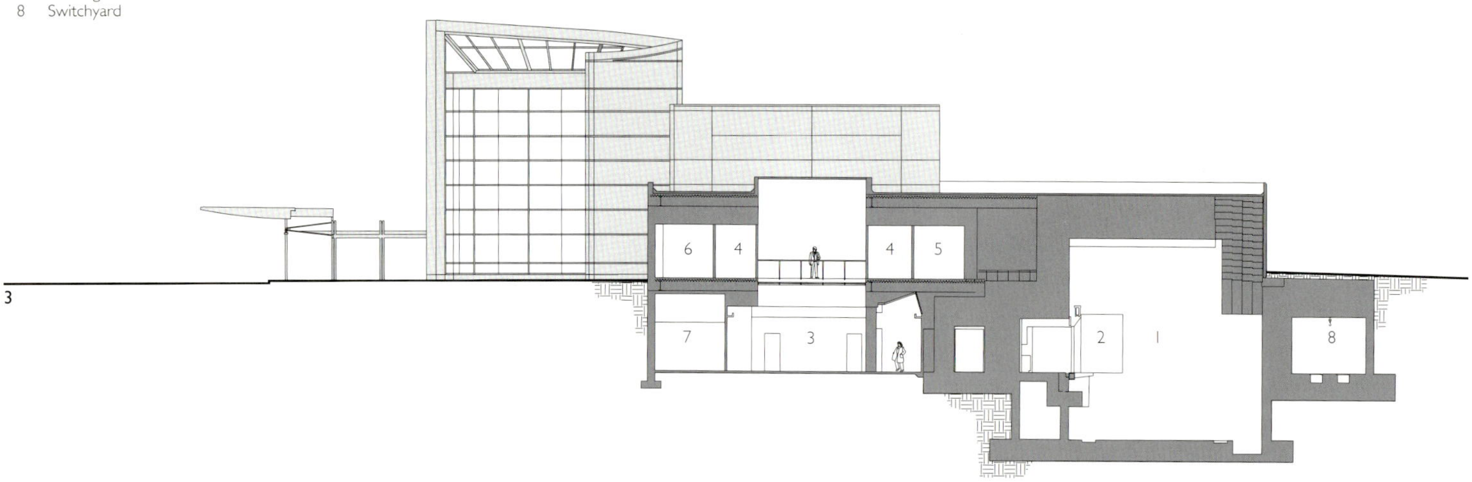

3

4

3 Section
4 Entry
5 Interior detail

5

1

2

Location	Burlington, Vermont
Completion	2005
Size	950,000 square feet

1 Concept sketch
2 Entry
3 Aerial
Following pages:
Medical Education Center Concourse

Fletcher Allen Health Care
Renaissance Project

3

The Renaissance Project is the largest healthcare development ever undertaken in the state of Vermont and represents the first phase of a three-part master plan to unite clinical, education, and research efforts on Fletcher Allen Health Care's main campus. This phase integrates an ambulatory care center, a medical education center and library, a central utilities plant, and an underground parking structure designed with a landscaped roof that provides a formal street-level approach to the main pavilion. The goal of the project was to enhance the delivery of first-class healthcare for residents of Vermont and upstate New York by establishing a clear sense of place, improving access through a single point of entry, and creating a meaningful connection with the natural environment.

Massed to create a major new campus quadrangle, the Renaissance Project eliminates the existing street barrier between hospital and medical school, pushing vehicular traffic away from pedestrian life to a ring road at the project's perimeter. Oriented toward spectacular views of the Green Mountains, Lake Champlain, and the Adirondacks, the ambulatory care center presents sweeping contemporary lines of stainless steel and glass curtainwall that work together to assert a dignified, confident façade. Details rendered in limestone and other natural finishes found elsewhere on the existing campus introduce warmth and resonate with the rural character of Vermont.

The ambulatory care center is designed to be patient-centered and operationally efficient. Two major atria bring natural light into the main building's core and offer a sense of connection with the outdoors. The lobby serves as a single point of entry for the entire facility, connecting ambulatory, diagnostic, and inpatient services, while the Medical Education Center acts as a symbolic and literal bridge between patient care, education, and research. The new physical integration between buildings has resulted in measurably increased efficiency for physicians who can now treat patients and perform other teaching or research duties without leaving the campus.

Opposite:
Approach from UVM campus
6 Site plan
7 Clinical atrium
8 Medical education library

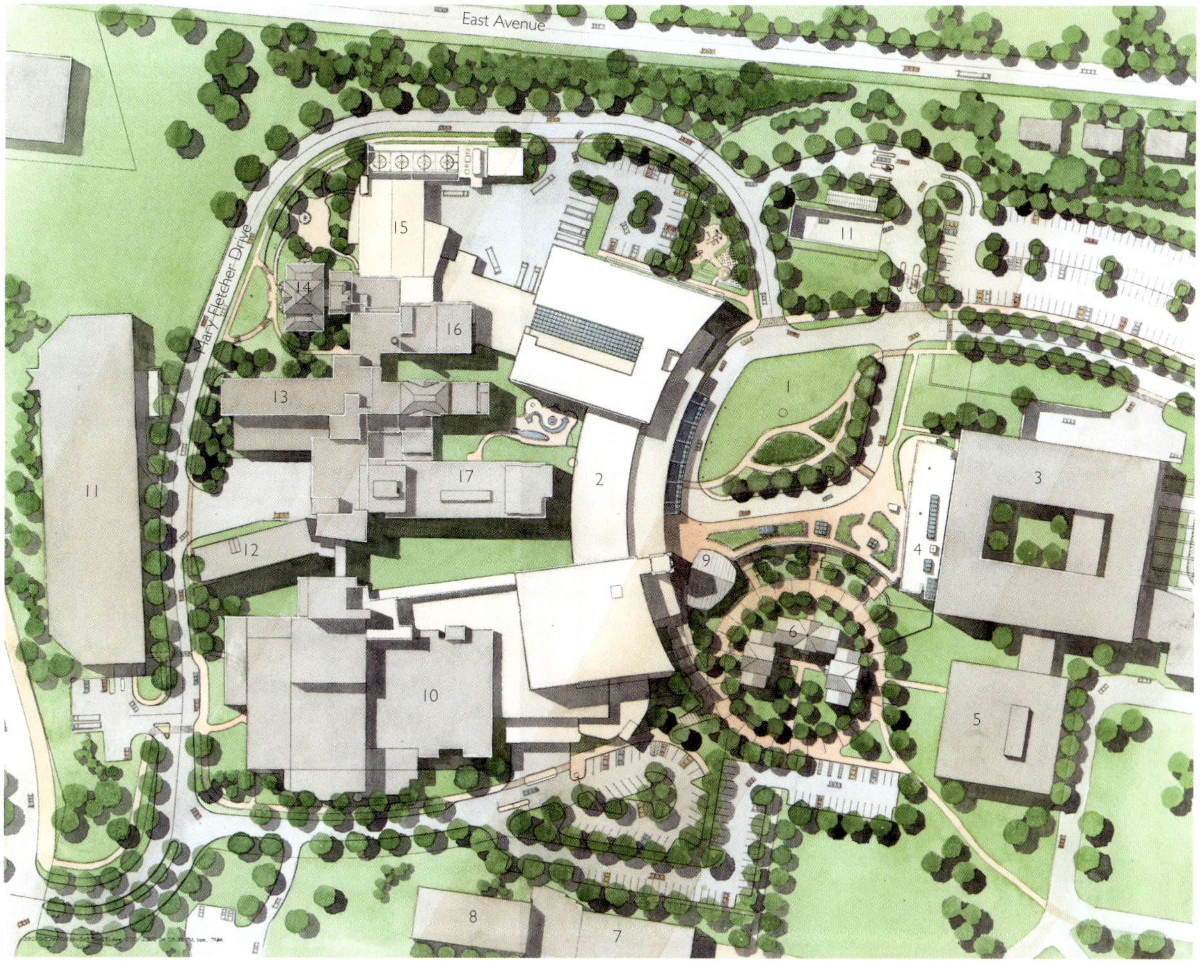

1 Entry quad
2 Ambulatory Care Center
3 Given Building
4 Medical Education Center
5 Rowell Hall
6 Converse Hall
7 Buckham Hall
8 Chittenden Hall
9 Auditorium
10 McClure Building
11 Parking
12 Patrick Building
13 Shepardson Building
14 Mary Fletcher Building
15 Central power plant
16 Engineering Building
17 Baird Building

6

7

8

9 Entry
10 Section
11 Patient Access Center waiting
12 Tower detail
13 Stone detail

9

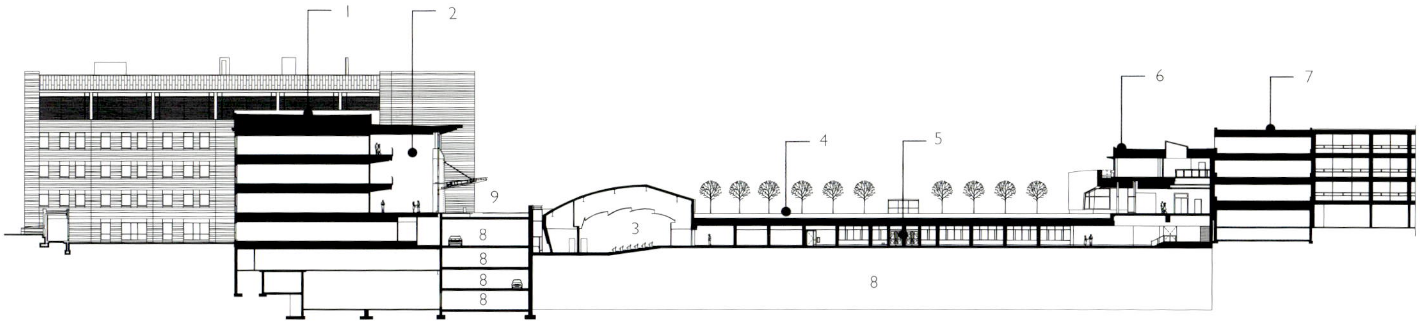

10

1 Ambulatory Care Center
2 Patient Access Center
3 Auditorium
4 Entry quad
5 Medical Education Center Concourse
6 Medical Education Center
7 Given Building
8 Parking
9 Drop-off

11

12

13

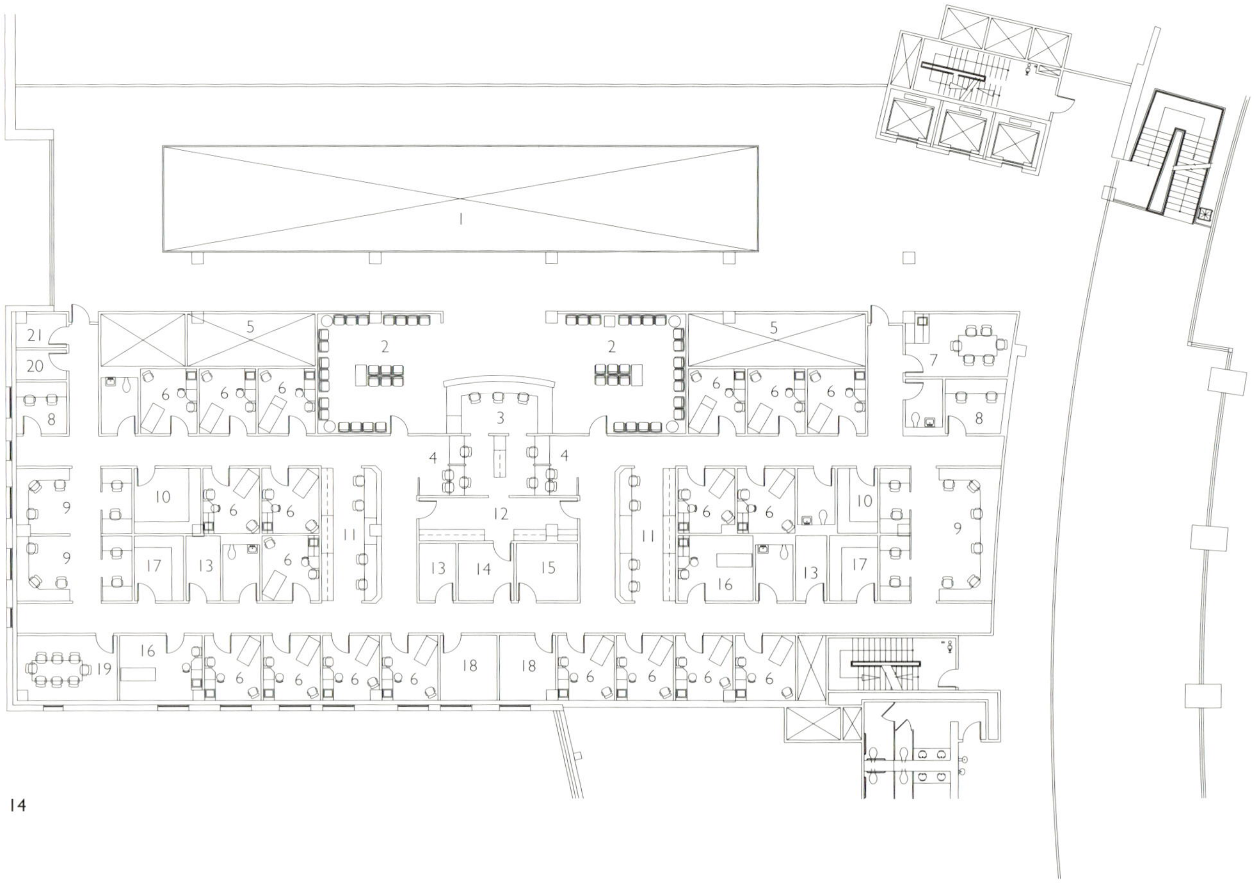

14

14 Typical clinical module
15 Medical Education Center auditorium
16 Main lobby
Opposite:
Clinical Care reception

1 Atrium (open to below)
2 Waiting
3 Reception
4 Checkout
5 Mechanical
6 Exam
7 Staff room
8 Triage
9 Work/dict
10 Clean holding
11 Team work
12 Work room
13 Storage
14 Medical records
15 Administration
16 Treatment
17 Soiled utility
18 Consulting
19 Conference
20 Soiled holding
21 Housekeeping

15

16

NEUROLOGY
AND
NEUROLOGICAL
SURGERY
SURGERY
OUTPATIENT CLINIC
EAST

1

1 Campus gateway
2 Surgical corridor
3 Emergency Department entrance

Location	Cleveland, Ohio
Completion	2004
Size	200,000 square feet

MetroHealth Medical Center

Critical Care Pavilion

2

3

The Critical Care Pavilion on MetroHealth Medical Center's main campus grew out of a multi-phased master plan developed for the hospital's East Campus. Located at the southern edge of the campus at the intersection of two major entrances, the Critical Care Pavilion serves as the campus gateway. It consolidates MetroHealth's Emergency and Perioperative Departments into a single Level One trauma center offering world-class services to upwards of 100,000 patients per year. The building also creates a new entry concourse that establishes the vehicular circulation pattern for the entire campus, and a separate ambulance court relieves traffic congestion and allows for the efficient queuing of emergency vehicles.

The exterior brick and glass curtainwall unites the architectural styles of existing campus buildings while establishing a new 21st-century aesthetic that suggests the advanced medical care provided within. The two-story, curved curtainwall façade on the building's southern edge offers users inside a visual connection to the outside world. The arcade on the building's north side corresponds with a pedestrian arcade associated with a nearby parking garage and adds a human scale to this important street edge.

A soaring three-and-one-half-story entry rotunda serves as the public lobby and primary circulation area, drawing light into the building's core. The curtainwall façade also brings abundant natural light into the building and offers staff and patients in the private clinical area a visual connection to the outdoors.

At street level, the emergency department includes 60 highly flexible exam rooms, state-of-the-art imaging, and the urgent care center. The first floor links back to the main hospital and houses the Perioperative Department, which includes 20 operating rooms that are organized by surgical specialty. A private internal corridor along the southern edge of the first floor features seating alcoves within the restricted zone where staff can rest and reflect. The second floor houses the mechanical penthouse that is outfitted to support a future four-floor intensive care unit expansion. Planning for the expansion also requires relocation of the helipad to accommodate the MetroHealth Life Flight system.

4 Site plan
5 Interior detail
6 Rotunda with bridge connection
Opposite:
Rotunda detail

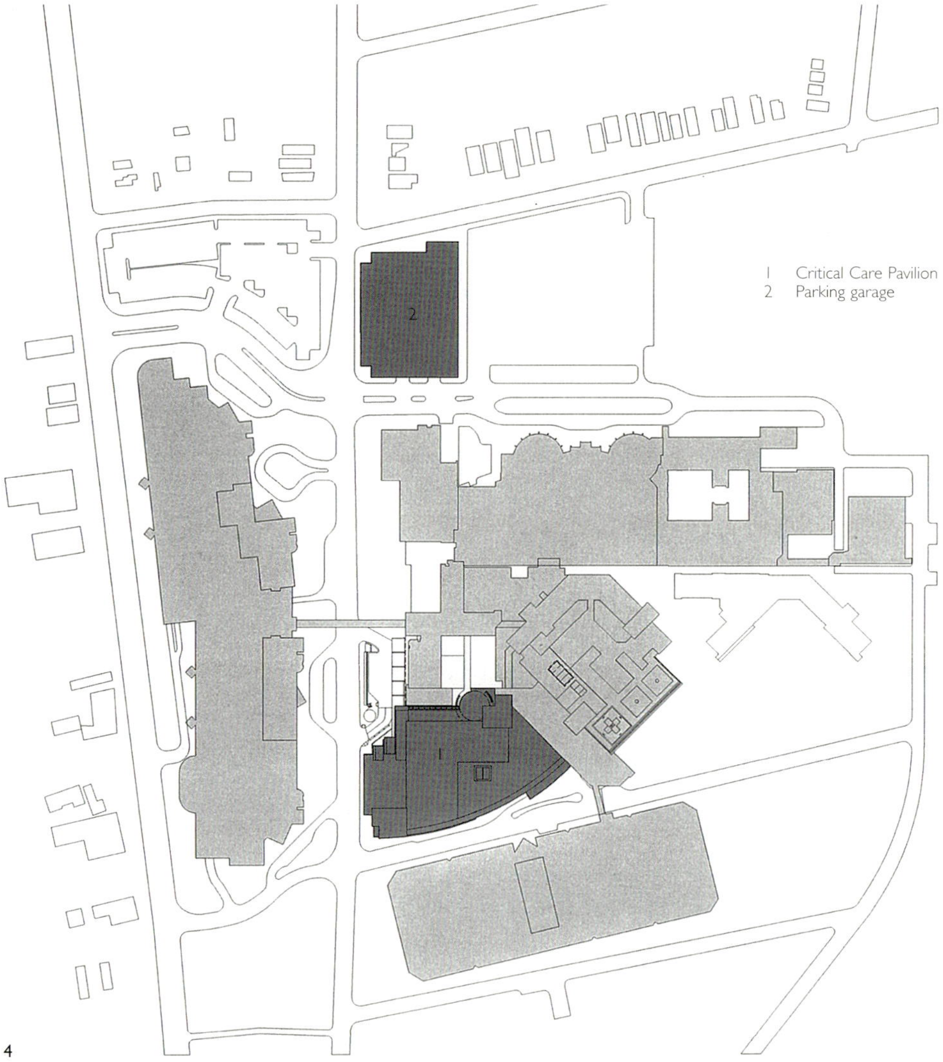

4

5

6

Location	Boston, Massachusetts
Completion	1998 construction complete
	2001 first patient treatment
Size	44,900 square feet

Opposite:
Façade detail
2 Reception
3 Patient treatment

Massachusetts General Hospital
Francis H. Burr Proton Therapy Center

2

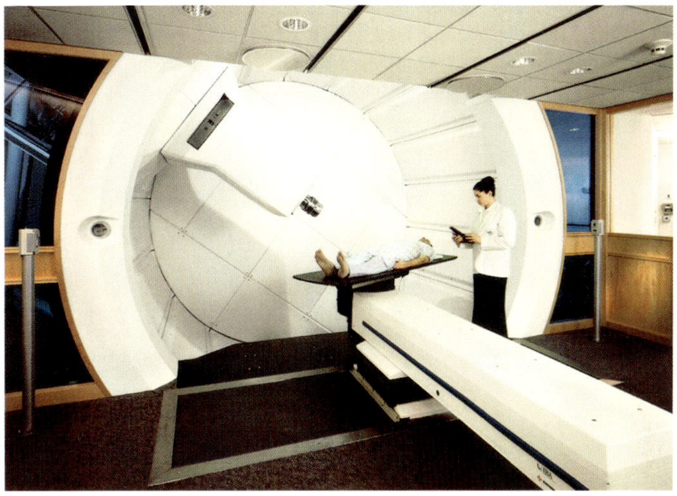

3

Based on cyclotron technology developed in the 1930s, proton therapy demands highly specialized equipment and spaces capable of providing both radiation shielding and extraordinary structural support. The Francis H. Burr Proton Therapy Center, just the second of its kind at the time it was built, welcomes patients and their families with a warm façade and interior waiting areas that are light-filled and calming. Built partially underground to take advantage of the earth's barrier against radiation, the building has enlivened a previously neglected urban street and helped spawn a new generation of proton treatment centers worldwide. Anticipating future growth, the building was designed to accommodate a possible third gantry as well as a planned expansion that was later constructed above it.

The exterior is rendered in blush-toned precast concrete, brushed aluminum, and glass—materials that are decidedly contemporary yet also respectful of the building's historical context. A monumental rotunda reinforces the street edge, recalling the cyclotron within and creating a generous entry where a halo of clerestory windows greets patients and their families and brings natural light into both the upper and lower levels of the building.

The rotunda's interior presents a compelling wall graphic that depicts a Bragg peak, the zenith of a proton beam's energy as it strikes the heart of a tumor. A sweeping stair leads to the subterranean level where a luminous corridor creates a friendly threshold to the treatment rooms—two gantry-style and one fixed-beam. Conventional doors belie the dense concrete walls necessary for shielding against radiation migration. The circular verticality of the building allows daylight to illuminate even its lowest levels, and the use of a bright, primary color scheme expresses the elemental nature of physics while creating a cheerful environment for patients, their families, and staff.

Location	Pittsburgh, Pennsylvania
Completion	1997
Size	365,000 square feet

Opposite:
Lobby
2 Entry pavilion

Magee-Womens Hospital of UPMC

Womancare Oakland

2

Located at the center of Magee-Womens Hospital of UPMC's existing campus, this building unites the hospital's east and west campuses and provides state-of-the-art facilities for leading programs in labor/delivery/recovery, breast cancer, infertility, menopause, teenage pregnancy, prenatal care, continuing education, and clinical research. Representing the first phase of a facilities master plan that addressed the shift from inpatient to outpatient care, the ambulatory care center expresses a forward-looking, elegant image that reflects Magee-Womens Hospital's commitment to excellence in women's healthcare.

A brightly illuminated entry pavilion simplifies front-door arrival and wayfinding. The pie-shaped plan organizes ambulatory, inpatient, and administrative functions. Separate staff and visitor circulation spines delineate on-stage (public) and off-stage (private) activities and spaces. Two landscaped courtyards introduce sunlight to the heart of the building. The entry pavilion, a multilevel atrium offering spectacular views to the Pittsburgh skyline, integrates the building's multiple corridors and levels and provides a clear organizational element for patients and visitors. A highly visible and accessible conference center located just off the pavilion reinforces Magee's role as a community resource by providing space for ongoing educational programs affiliated with the hospital as well as for meetings of various women-focused Pittsburgh organizations.

Key diagnostic and support functions are centralized on the building's lower levels. On the upper floors, medical office suites are grouped around the multilevel atrium to ease patient access and aid in orientation. Wood-and-glass partitions in the clinic waiting areas open onto the atrium, bringing natural light into the suites and making occupants aware of activity in the lobby below while shielding them from the public to maximize privacy. Lighting, finishes and interior details work together to create spaces that provide intimate havens for patients and staff within the building's relatively large footprint.

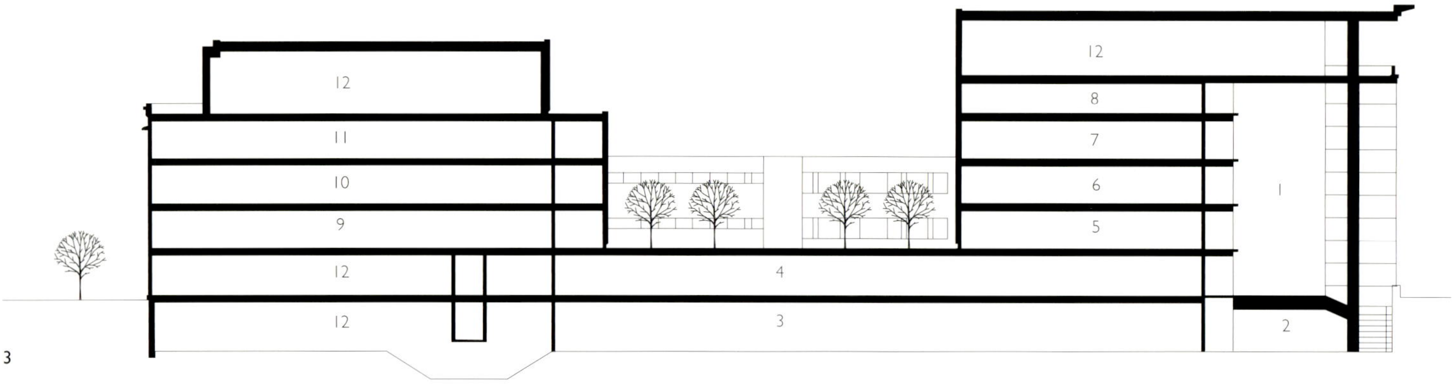

3

1	Lobby	7	Breast center
2	Conference center	8	Oncology
3	Radiation oncology	9	Labor/delivery/recovery
4	Admitting	10	Surgery
5	Prenatal monitoring	11	Clinical labs
6	Surgery faculty	12	Building services

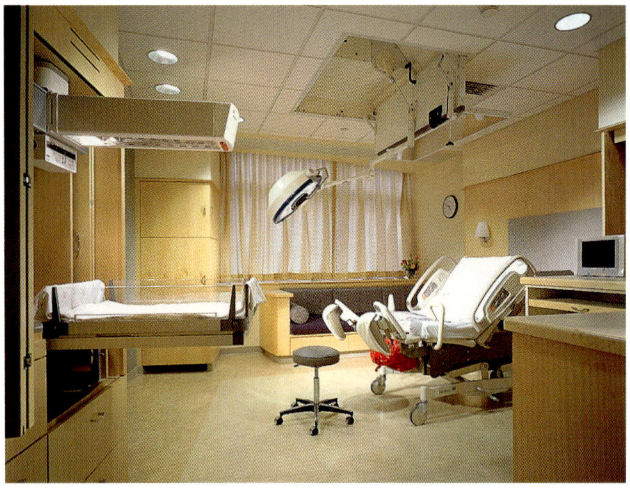

4

5

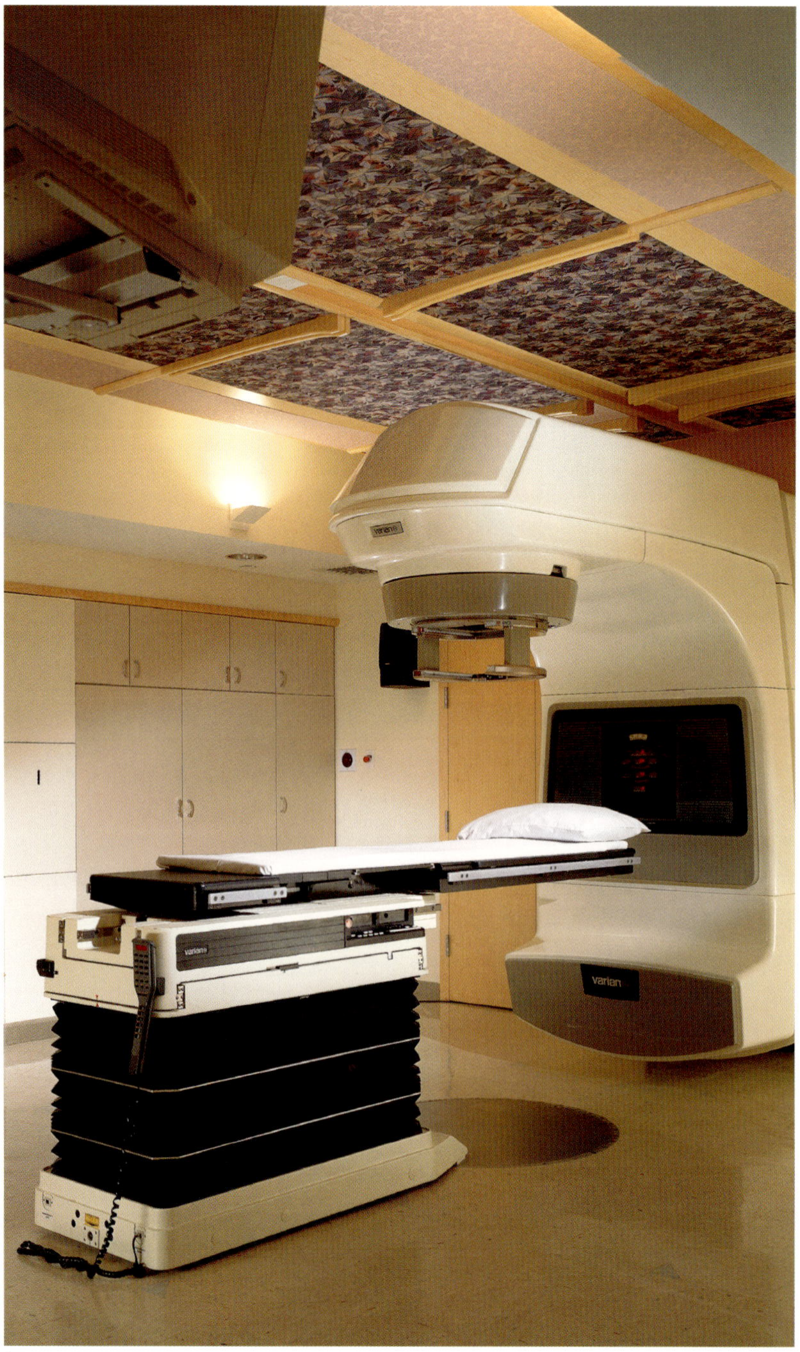

6

3 North–south section
4 Labor/delivery/recovery
5 Conference center
6 Treatment room
7 Entry canopy

7

8

8 Atrium
9 Site plan
10 Northwest façade

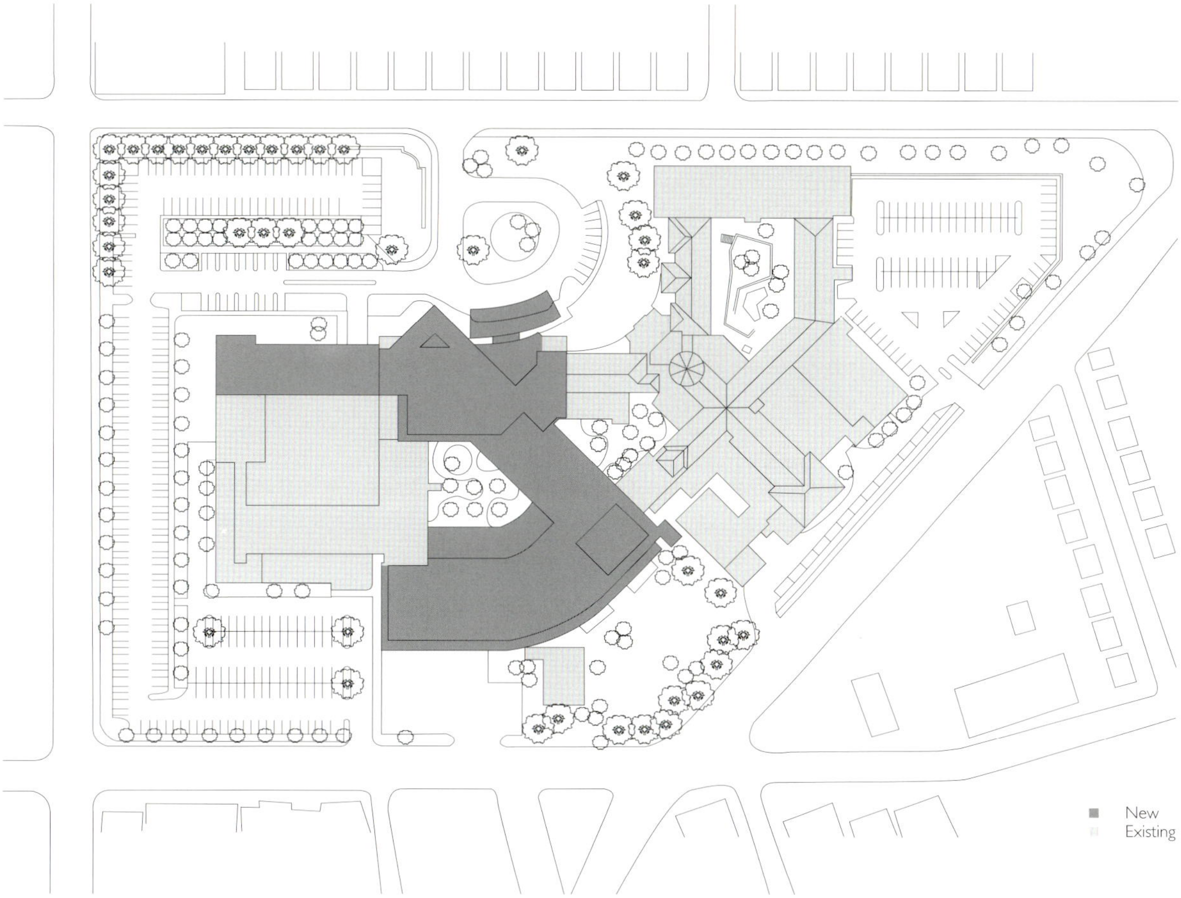

9

10

Location	Chicago, Illinois
Completion	1997
Size	520,000 square feet

University of Chicago Hospitals

Duchossois Center for Advanced Medicine

Opposite:
Façade detail
2 Entry tower

2

The Duchossois Center for Advanced Medicine represents a new model of clinical practice for this major academic medical center, providing a one-stop destination for outpatient care and an ambulatory teaching environment to accommodate the university's leading medical education program. The project grew out of a two-year master planning effort to evaluate whether the existing 2.1-million-square-foot campus shared by the University of Chicago Hospitals and Pritzker School of Medicine could respond to changes in healthcare delivery methodology and medical education pedagogy.

Consolidating ambulatory services on a highly visible site in a dense inner-city neighborhood, the building interacts comfortably with the traditional Gothic style found elsewhere on the university's campus. Also at home among the Miesian Modernism that is prevalent throughout Chicago, the building assumes an independent identity that is both contemporary and suggestive of future design trends. The facility is made up of two carefully massed six-story blocks that flank a series of central atria bounded at either end by two signature towers that identify the building's major entrances. The atria admit daylight and mitigate the large floor plates.

The exterior is rendered in warm-toned precast concrete panels mixed with regional limestone chips, evoking the neighboring limestone buildings. Multistory curtainwall panels and tapered precast concrete piers express rhythm and articulate the building's Gothic counterparts. A second-level bridge and curved glass canopy animate the main entrance. The facility's interior is characterized by spacious and flexible floor plates that enable a variety of clinical modules and sub-specialties to share practice space, systems, and amenities, resulting in enhanced efficiency and the creation an "ideal patient encounter."

A four-story atrium is surrounded by the major public circulation corridors and waiting areas that connect the ambulatory suites to the west with the diagnostic and treatment programs to the east. A skylight and the glass curtainwall enclosure bring natural light into the building's core and offer orienting views to the surrounding urban landscape and the downtown Chicago skyline. The contemporary Gothic motif is carried throughout the interior details and finishes. Colored stone, rich woods such as cherry and mahogany, and patterned terrazzo floors reinforce a feeling of comfort and patient-centered care.

3 East façade
Opposite:
Bridge detail

3

DO NOT
ENTER

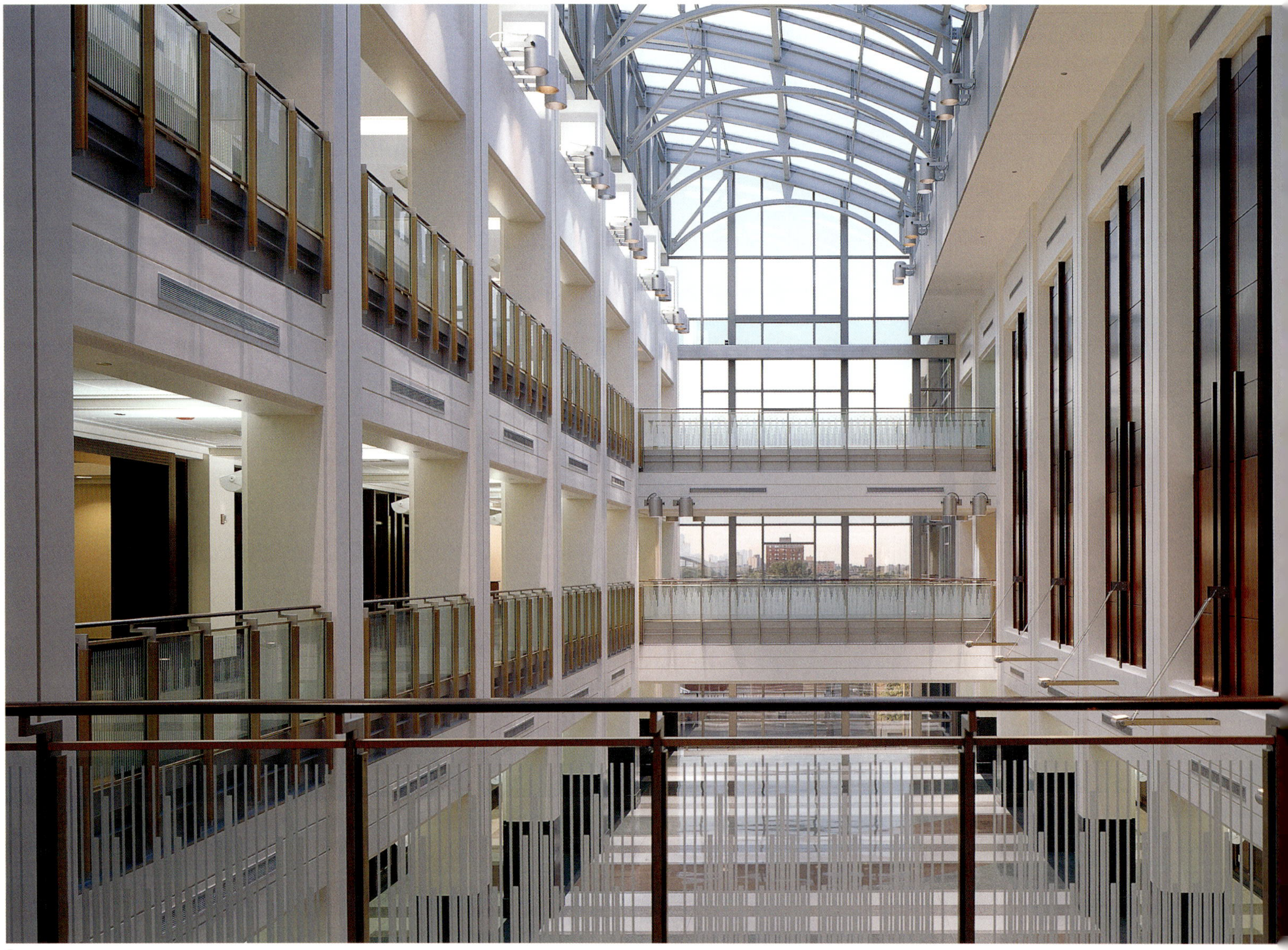

5

6

5 Atrium
6 Reception desk
7 Entry level floor plan
8 Typical floor plan

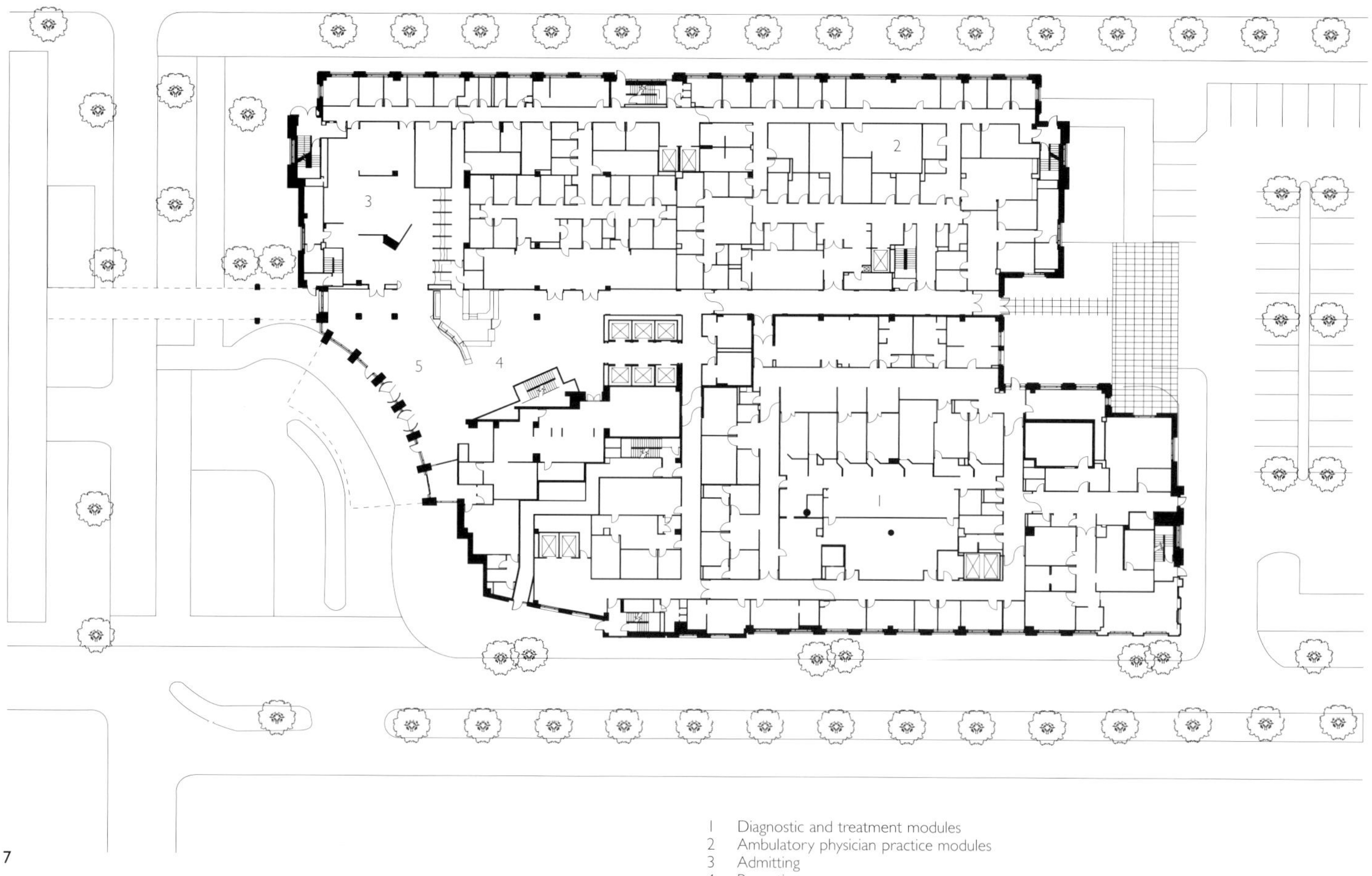

7

1 Diagnostic and treatment modules
2 Ambulatory physician practice modules
3 Admitting
4 Reception
5 Lobby

8

1 Diagnostic and treatment modules
2 Ambulatory physician practice modules
3 Reception
4 Waiting

Location	Boston, Massachusetts
Completion	1994
Size	265,000 square feet

Opposite:
Typical module
2 Campus integration

Brigham and Women's Hospital
Center for Women and Newborns

2

The Center for Women and Newborns represents the culmination of more than 10 years of strategic planning, programming, and facilities master planning at Brigham and Women's Hospital. One of the earliest prototypes for developing active labor management and for establishing a single standard of care regardless of a patient's economic status, the facility is home to the world's first interventional iMR suite, reasserting Brigham and Women's as a world leader in healthcare.

The 12-story building consolidates services that were previously scattered across the campus, enabling the hospital to respond to a surge in demand for obstetric care. Through careful, restrained massing and thoughtful materials choice for the building skin, the Center for Women and Newborns unifies the surrounding architectural diversity and strengthens the campus' varied urban character.

Accessed from a ¼-mile-long internal circulation spine called "The Pike," the two-story lobby is a light-filled destination that serves as the building entry. Entrances to the facility's four major clinics are immediately visible from the reception area of the adjacent ambulatory suite, making wayfinding an intuitive and low-stress experience for patients and visitors.

From its graceful, curved ceiling supported by grand columns to its richly composed floors and use of color-saturated fabrics, the building's lobby creates a warm but expansive and welcoming environment. Many of the exterior materials, colors, and patterns are repeated inside, providing an immediate sense of orientation and continuity throughout the building.

The Center for Women and Newborns is designed to respond to the personal—not just the medical—needs of patients and their families.

Leading an increasingly popular trend, the facility was the first in Massachusetts to provide only private rooms in the labor, delivery, and postpartum suites. Taking cues from the hospitality field, the building also offers abundant natural light, easy access to the outdoors, and family space. Throughout the building, technology is largely hidden from view behind custom finishes and furnishings as well as artwork. Separate areas for families and staff contribute to an overall atmoshere of comfort and dignity.

In the neonatal intensive care unit (NICU), larger nurseries provide more room for visiting parents. Overnight rooms help parents of babies who are nearly ready to leave the hospital prepare for life at home. Just steps away, a sunny and inviting rooftop solarium, an outdoor terrace, and comfortable lounges offer spaces for quiet retreat.

3

Center for Women & Newborns
Center for Women & Newborns
BIMA
Ambulatory Services Lobby

4

3 Bridge detail
4 Atrium from "The Pike"
5 Section
6 Labor/delivery/recovery waiting

1 iMR suite
2 Anesthesiology
3 Emergency
4 Lobby
5 The Pike
6 Women's Health Center
7 OB/Gyn outpatient services
8 Labor/delivery/recovery staff support
9 Labor/delivery/recovery
10 NICU
11 Postpartum
12 Shell
13 Mechanical

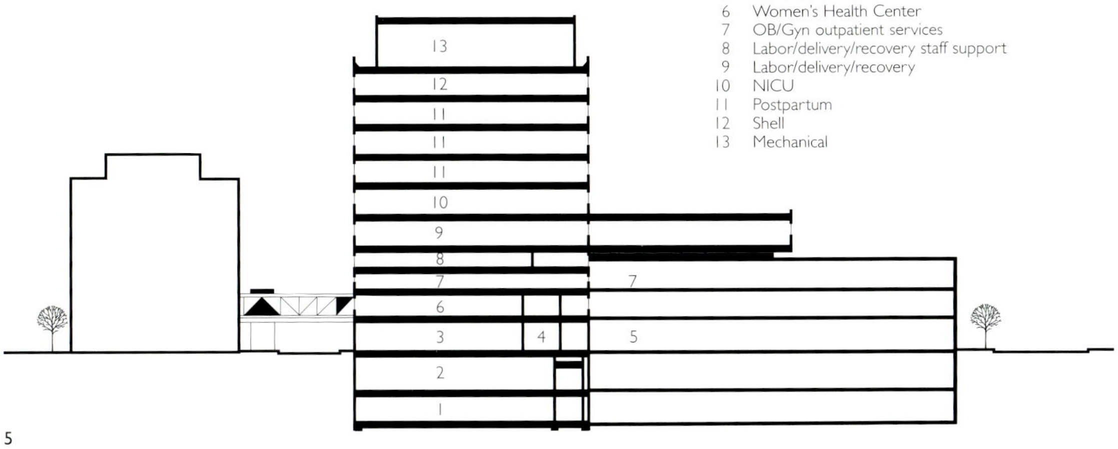

5

6

- The Pike
1 Entry
2 Patient tower
3 Tower lobby
4 Center for Women and Newborns
5 Ambulatory I
6 Ambulatory II
7 Tackaberry Building
8 Peter Bent Brigham Hospital
9 Medical research building

7

8

9

10

11

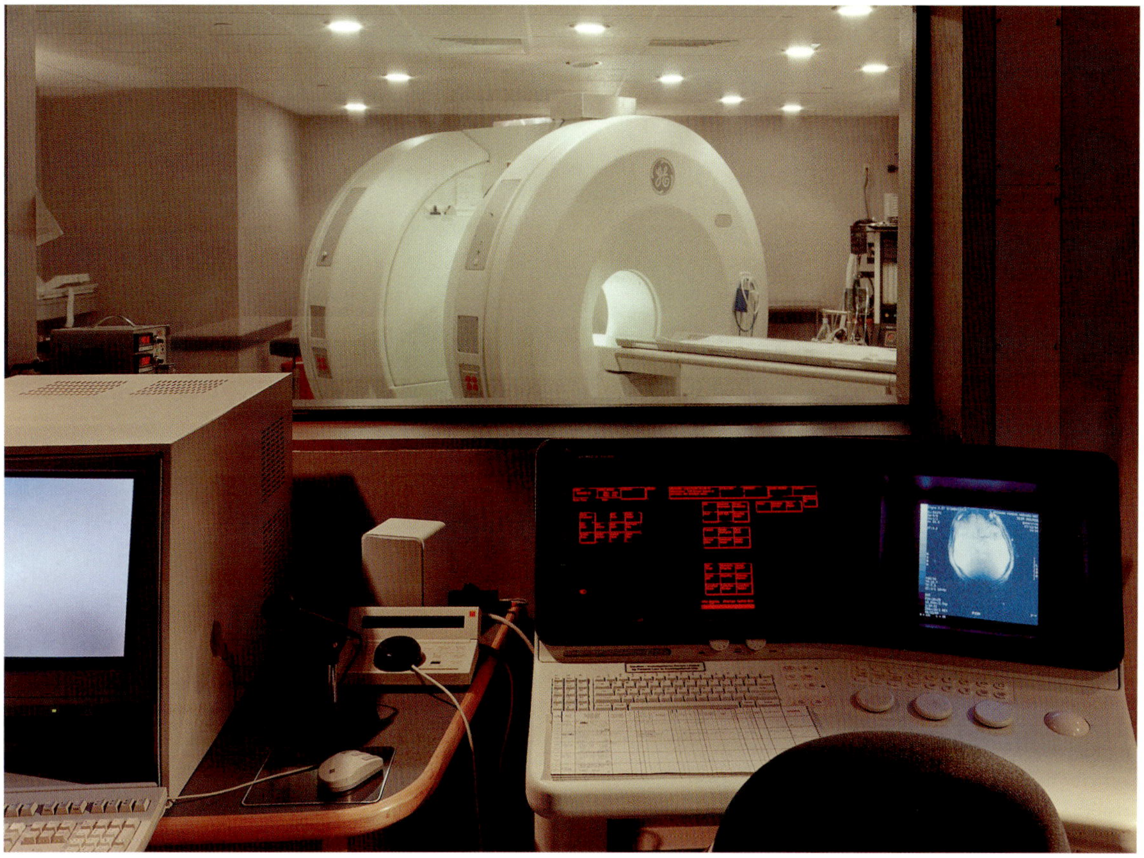

12

11 Postpartum corridor
12 iMR suite

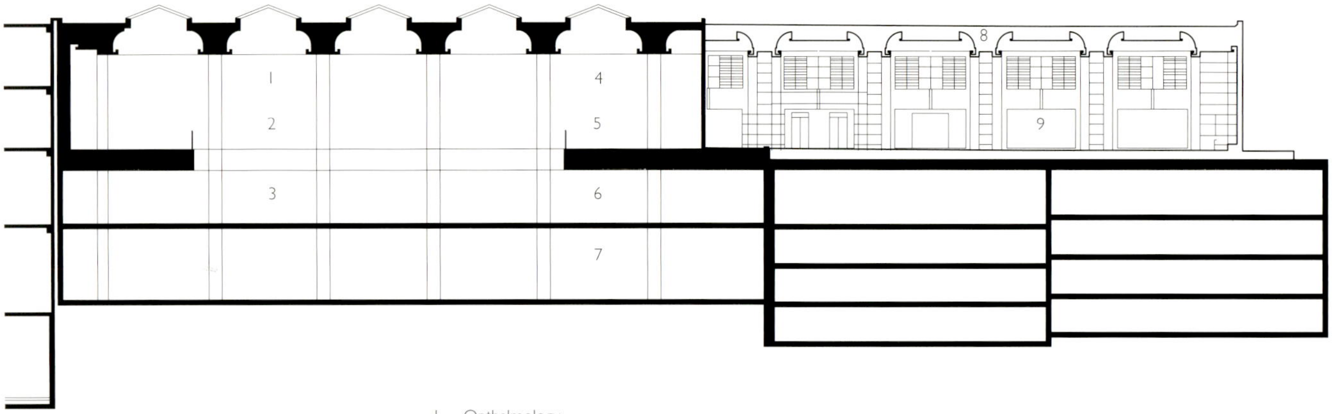

1

1 Opthalmology
2 Dental
3 Ambulatory Radiology
4 Urology
5 Registration
6 Orthopedics/Rheumatology
7 MRI
8 Atrium beyond
9 Entrance plaza

2

Location	Boston, Massachusetts
Completion	1987
Size	114,300 square feet

1 Section
2 Street façade
3 Lobby

Brigham and Women's Hospital
Ambulatory Services Building II

3

Part of a master plan aimed at reorganizing and rebuilding to improve Brigham and Women's Hospital's operational efficiency, outpatient care capacity, and public image, this ambulatory care facility plays a key role in unifying a previously fractured urban campus. The facility was designed to promote a single standard of care, and establishes a new model for ambulatory teaching environments. A standardized exam module enhances throughput and co-location of clinical exam modules, and corresponding diagnostic and treatment services facilitate a seamless, one-stop service for patients and families.

Two of the four treatment levels, as well as a four-story garage, are built underground to allow the facility to maintain a sympathetic scale with a block of houses just across the street and optimize functional relationships to key diagnostic and treatment areas in the adjoining hospital. Sited in a neighborhood that is dense with diverse medical facilities, the building's residential feeling is further promoted by a uniform series of bow-fronted façades evocative of traditional Boston row houses.

The Brigham and Women's campus is chiefly organized around its primary pedestrian circulation spine, a ¼-mile-long corridor known as "The Pike." Revitalizing this important hub was a key goal of the project. The Ambulatory Services Building II features a skylit 300-foot-long atrium lobby that parallels the mid-portion of The Pike, offering alternative avenues for patient and visitor traffic while providing an open, thoughtfully detailed space for impromptu staff interactions. The well-lit atrium serves as the primary ambulatory entrance to the hospital and is easily identified from the street.

All of the clinical departments are accessed through the atrium, and its numerous small seating alcoves provide more intimately scaled waiting areas for the physicians' suites that overlook it. Tall bay windows provide views to the entry plaza and drop-off area outside while its proximity to the entrance, garage elevator, and research and administrative facilities make the luminous atrium a preferred location for staff meetings, seminars, and public gatherings.

Opposite:
Atrium
5 Entry level plan
6 Radiology
7 Waiting

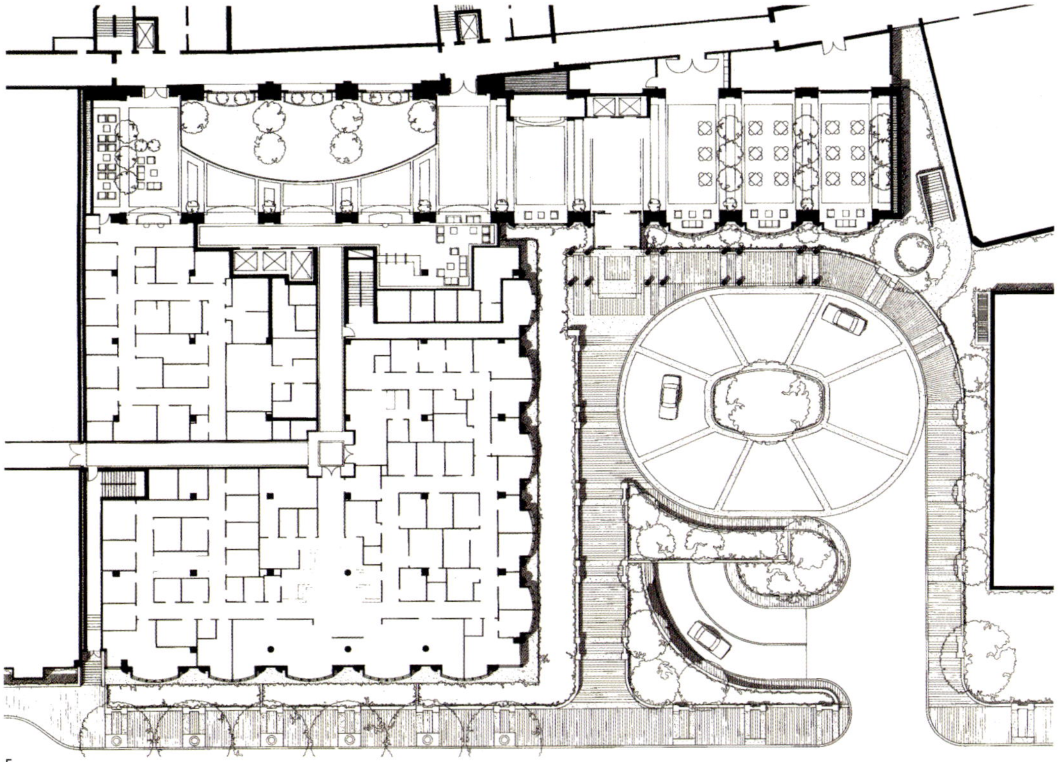

5

6

7

Science and Technology

Location	Boston, Massachusetts
Completion	2008
Size	777,600 square feet

Opposite:
Façade detail
2 Multipurpose gallery

Lyme Properties | BioMed Realty Trust

Center for Life Science Boston

2

The Center for Life Science Boston is the first of its kind in the country. A speculative, privately owned, multi-tenant laboratory building, it offers much-needed, flexible, cutting-edge research space to leading academic and medical institutions—Beth Israel Deaconess Medical Center, the Dana-Farber Cancer Institute, Children's Hospital Boston, and the Immune Disease Institute—without the institutions having to spend their own capital dollars. The 20-story building is located in the Blackfan Research District of Boston's renowned Longwood Medical Area, home to the greatest concentration of academic medical researchers in the world.

Distinguished but not disruptive to the densely developed urban fabric, the building brings a signature presence to the Blackfan Research District, subdividing an existing super block while improving pedestrian and circulation amenities throughout. The generous setback of the building from Blackfan Circle relieves the dense street wall while its bifurcated massing minimizes its visual impact. The footprint increases as the building rises, making it appear less overwhelming to pedestrians. A series of external and internal pedestrian footpaths completes a vital connection to nearby mass transit hubs. On the ground level, a two-story, multipurpose gallery, combined with access to public amenities and below-grade parking, creates opportunities for interaction among the building's occupants and visitors from adjacent institutions.

The building's glass curtainwall façade is expressed though a dynamic interplay of planes, curves, and notches that evoke the optimistic but challenging research taking place within. These rhythmically organized details animate the exterior and announce the various points of entry. During the day, the façade maintains a high degree of transparency while subtly reflecting the daylight and sky. At night, the building is illuminated dramatically, creating a luminous focal point for the Blackfan District.

The Center for Life Science Boston is one of the first buildings accepted to the U.S. Green Building Council's LEED Core and Shell Pilot Project and has received gold pre-certification. At 289 feet, it is the tallest building in the Longwood area and one of the tallest research laboratory facilities in the United States. Though it can be seen from almost anywhere in Boston, the building conveys a human scale at the pedestrian level, due to the openness of its base and the paving that ties it to green space across the street. Far from the fortress-like image that characterizes many other research buildings of its scale, the Center for Life Science Boston achieves an overall effect of integration and connection between interior and exterior environments and public and private enterprise, and among education, research, and clinical care.

3 View from Blackfan Circle
4 Site plan with public circulation
5 Laboratory

3

Public circulation
1 Center for Life Science Boston
2 Center for Life Science Boston II
3 Karp Family Research Laboratories
4 Beth Israel Deaconess Medical Center
5 Merck
6 Harvard Institutes of Medicine
7 Harvard Medical School
8 Brigham and Women's Hospital
9 Dana-Farber Cancer Institute
10 Joslin Diabetes Center
11 Children's Hospital Boston main campus

4

5

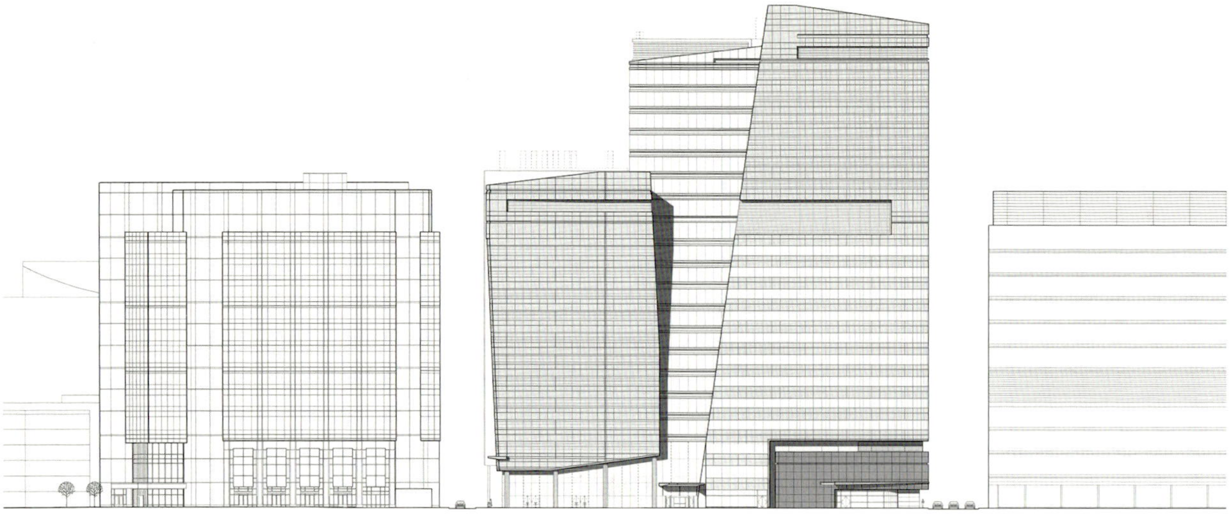

6

1 Harvard-affiliated institution TBD
2 Children's Hospital Boston
3 Dana-Farber Cancer Institute
4 Beth Israel Deaconess Medical Center
5 Immune Disease Institute
6 Retail
7 Mechanical
8 Parking
9 Support

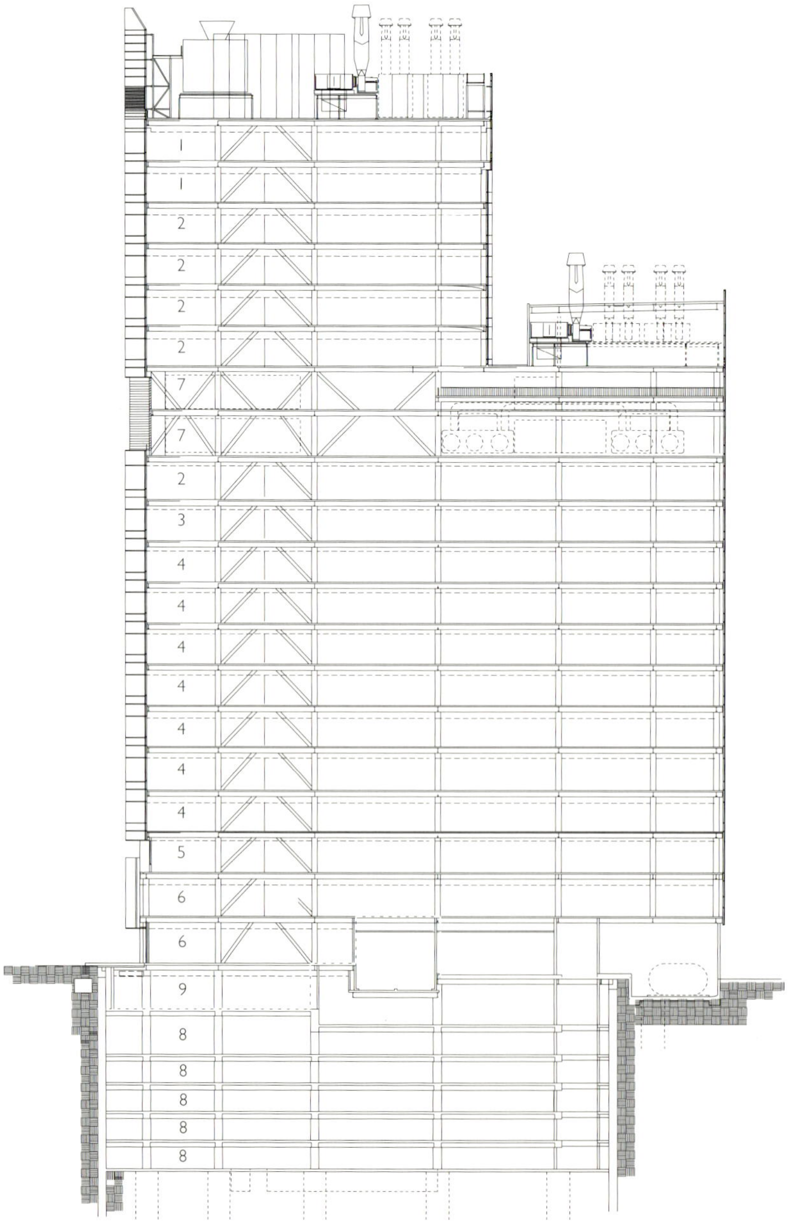

7

6 East elevation
7 Section
8 View from Brookline Avenue
9 Model
10 Concept sketch
Following pages:
Blackfan Circle façade

8

9

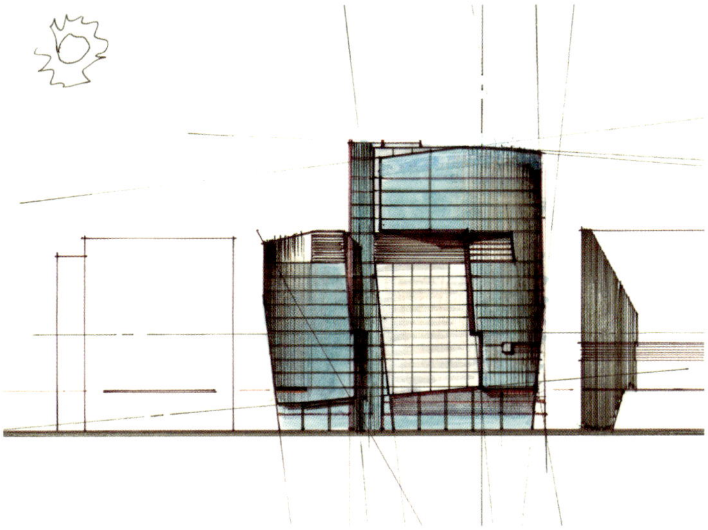

10

Location	Boston, Massachusetts
Completion	2003
Size	296,000 square feet

Opposite:
View from Blackfan Circle
2 Atrium

Children's Hospital Boston

Karp Family Research Laboratories

2

This laboratory building for one of the world's leading pediatric clinical and research institutions occupies a site in the heart of Boston's densely developed Longwood Medical Area, which is home to more than 4 million square feet of research space. The 12-story facility doubles Children's Hospital Boston's research space in the Longwood area and supports scientific and clinical investigators in various fields including cardiology, oncology, neurology, neonatology, orthopedics, and genetics. The laboratory also bolsters the hospital's efforts to attract top-notch talent and secure major funding from both government and private sources.

The building sits atop a five-level, below-grade parking garage, and forges a link with the existing hospital campus through its strong orientation to Longwood Avenue, the hospital's main address. Four stacked atria of three stories each provide a visual connection to the main campus and urban neighborhood while creating a physical identity for the research institutes. The exterior forms recognize the geometry of Longwood Avenue and Blackfan Circle.

The open, communal atria allow views of floors above and below while also providing delineated spaces that promote both socialization and quiet contemplation. The high transparency of the facility reinforces Children's Hospital Boston's strategy to create an environment that supports collaboration and interaction across scientific disciplines.

Lab floor layouts provide maximum usage flexibility to support organizational growth and change. Typically organized to include rows of labs, alcoves, a linear equipment room, lab support, and administrative offices, each space can be configured to accommodate various group sizes and customized to meet specific research requirements. Wet bench space is uniform on each floor and major corridors between the labs and offices, delineated by bright color palettes, are well-lit by natural and other light sources to produce an overall effect of openness to discovery and the free sharing of knowledge.

3 Interaction space
4 Laboratory
5 Site plan

3

4

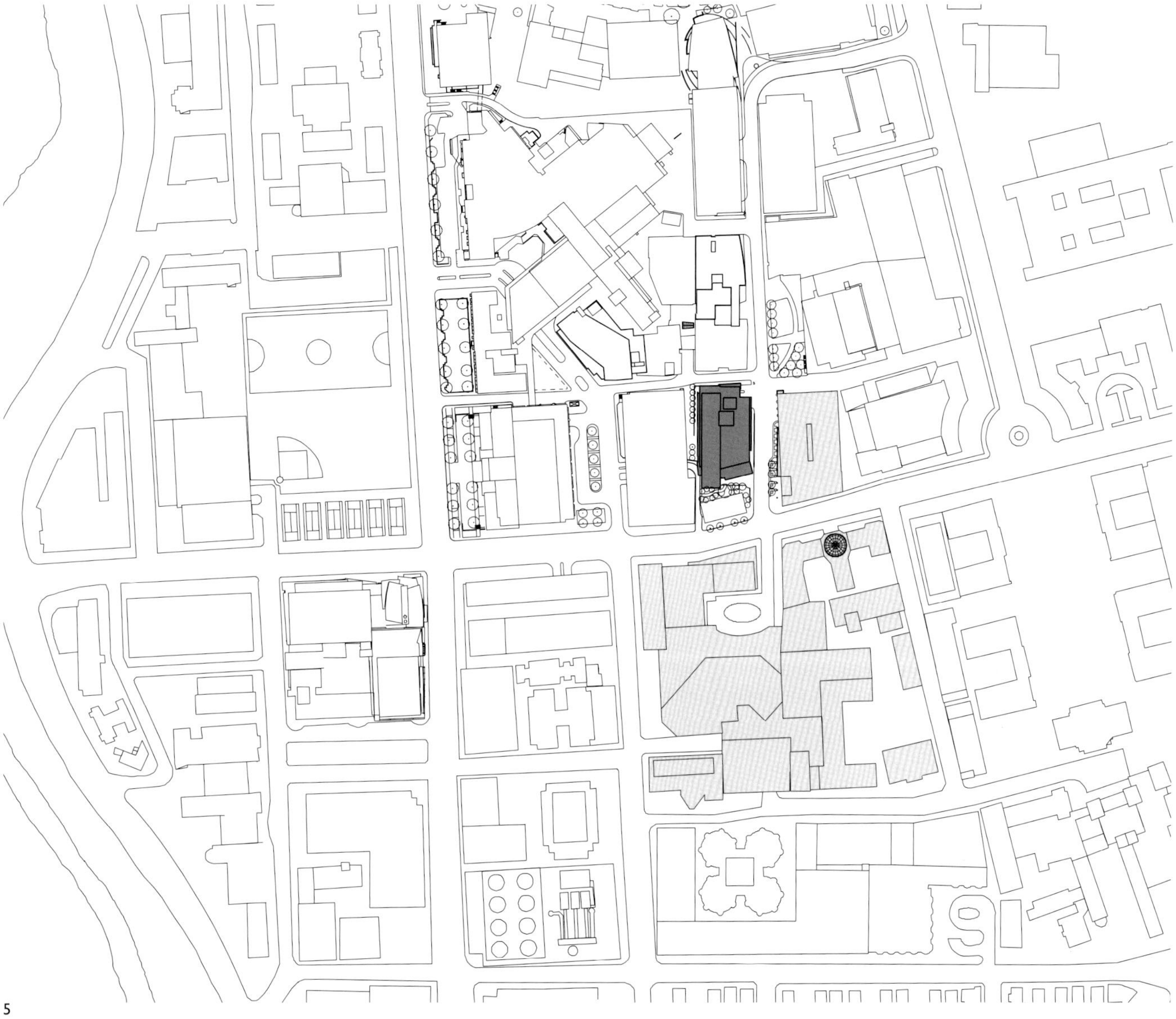

5

■ Karp Family Research Laboratories
// Children's Hospital Boston Campus

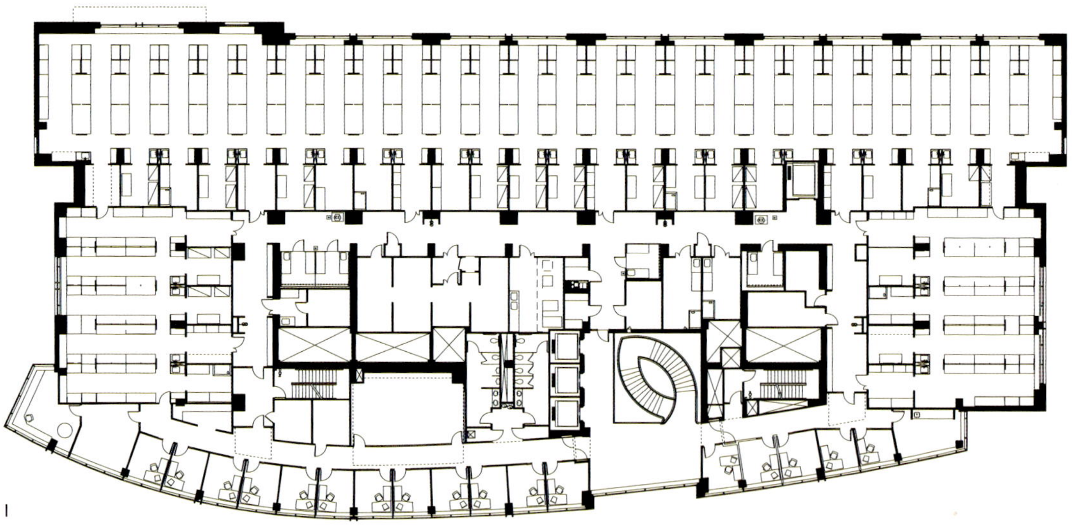

1

2

Location	Worcester, Massachusetts
Completion	2001
Size	360,000 square feet

1 Typical floor plan
2 Interaction space
3 Quadrangle view

University of Massachusetts Medical School

Aaron Lazare Medical Research Building

3

The first significant building project at the University of Massachusetts Medical School in nearly 30 years, the Aaron Lazare Medical Research Building expands the capacity for integrated education, research, and clinical health sciences on this campus by 60 percent. The state-of-the-art facility houses a cancer center, the departments of Medicine, Neurobiology, Biochemistry, and Molecular Biology, and programs focused on genetics and comparative medicine. The signature building represents a new era in research at UMass Medical School and has helped to position the university more competitively among its peers.

Light-colored precast concrete and glass curtainwall create a rhythmic skin in compelling contrast to the dark granite of the medical center and other existing campus buildings. Sited to create a corner to the central campus quadrangle, the facility casts a strong contemporary gesture against the skyline while at street level it defines the main campus open space. A zipper of glass runs up the front of the building to expose a trio of atria and accentuate the faculty lounge behind the building's brow.

Grouped around the atria, interior research zones, or neighborhoods, provide a visual and functional connection between floors and also offer places for staff and visitors to interact and relax. The first atrium includes the main building entry, elevator lobby, dining room, and a second-floor bridge to the rest of the campus. Each of the upper atria offers informal conference space and a monumental stair that is shaped to evoke the double-helix structure of DNA.

To encourage building users to circulate throughout the entire facility, core functions are dispersed on several floors. The west-facing side of the building houses generically rendered lab space that can be customized by users. Shared labs are located at the center of typical floor plates, with nearby alcoves available to encourage collaboration and promote a sense of community. Professional and administrative offices, which are clustered along the east-facing side of the building, enjoy lake views.

4

5

6

4 Connecting stair
5 Dining room
6 Laboratory

1 Marine Resources Center
2 Marine Resources Center corridor
3 Marine Resources Center laboratory

1

Location	Woods Hole, Massachusetts
Completion	1992-2007
Size	34,000 square feet (Marine Resources Center)
	32,035 square feet (Starr Building)
	33,000 square feet (Rowe Laboratory)

Marine Biological Laboratory

Marine Resources Center
C.V. Starr Environmental Sciences Building
Rowe Laboratory

2

3

Located in the historic seaside village of Woods Hole, the Marine Biological Laboratory is an international center for research, education, and training in biology, biomedicine, and ecology. The Marine Biological Laboratory's reputation as a global leader in marine research, combined with respect for the existing campus aesthetic and sensitivity to community concerns, have guided the design of new and renovated projects throughout the campus.

The state-of-the-art Marine Resources Center is the first facility of its kind in the United States with technology that enables marine organisms to live under ideal conditions. The design carefully integrates the building mass and scale into the existing campus and historic context. Access to the waterfront is maintained and landscaping invites area residents to enjoy the building's surroundings and its water views. Bay windows along the street side of the first floor allow passersby to observe small sharks, dog fish, horseshoe crabs, and other marine animals in their tanks.

The L-configuration of the Marine Resources Center responds to tight site constraints. The exterior is clad with granite and cast stone, materials that match the adjacent whaling-era building and provide protection from seawater migration, salt spray, and harsh winds. Custom-made large-paned windows and a pitched roof minimize the perceived scale of the building. Interior finishes were selected to withstand constant humidity and heavy use.

The design of the Marine Resources Center incorporates two distinct zones—wet and dry—to enable efficient vertical distribution of water. The ground floor is devoted to live-animal storage tanks. The second floor contains laboratories and classrooms. The third floor houses additional laboratory space, offices, and water storage tanks as well as mechanical equipment for the marine life support system.

The C.V. Starr Environmental Sciences Building, the second major new construction project on the Marine Biological Laboratory campus since the 1970s, responds to a six-fold growth in the Ecosystems Center, a globally focused multidisciplinary research program. Uniting the staff under a single roof, the facility nearly doubles the Center's previous space and introduces modern laboratories, classrooms, and conference facilities. Opening onto an intimately scaled and richly landscaped quadrangle, the Starr Building completes a complex of facilities that form the heart of the Marine Biological Laboratory's research effort and academic campus.

The renovation and expansion of the Rowe Laboratory, formerly known as the Whitman Building, constitutes the first significant upgrade to the facility since it was built in 1960. Equipping the building to meet 10-year growth projections while accommodating leading-edge science required gutting, modernizing, and upgrading the interior to adhere to current safety standards. The highly scalable design incorporates modular labs with temporary walls that can be added or removed to allow for expansion or contraction without any disruption to building systems. Laboratories are situated on the exterior walls to take advantage of natural light and Woods Hole views.

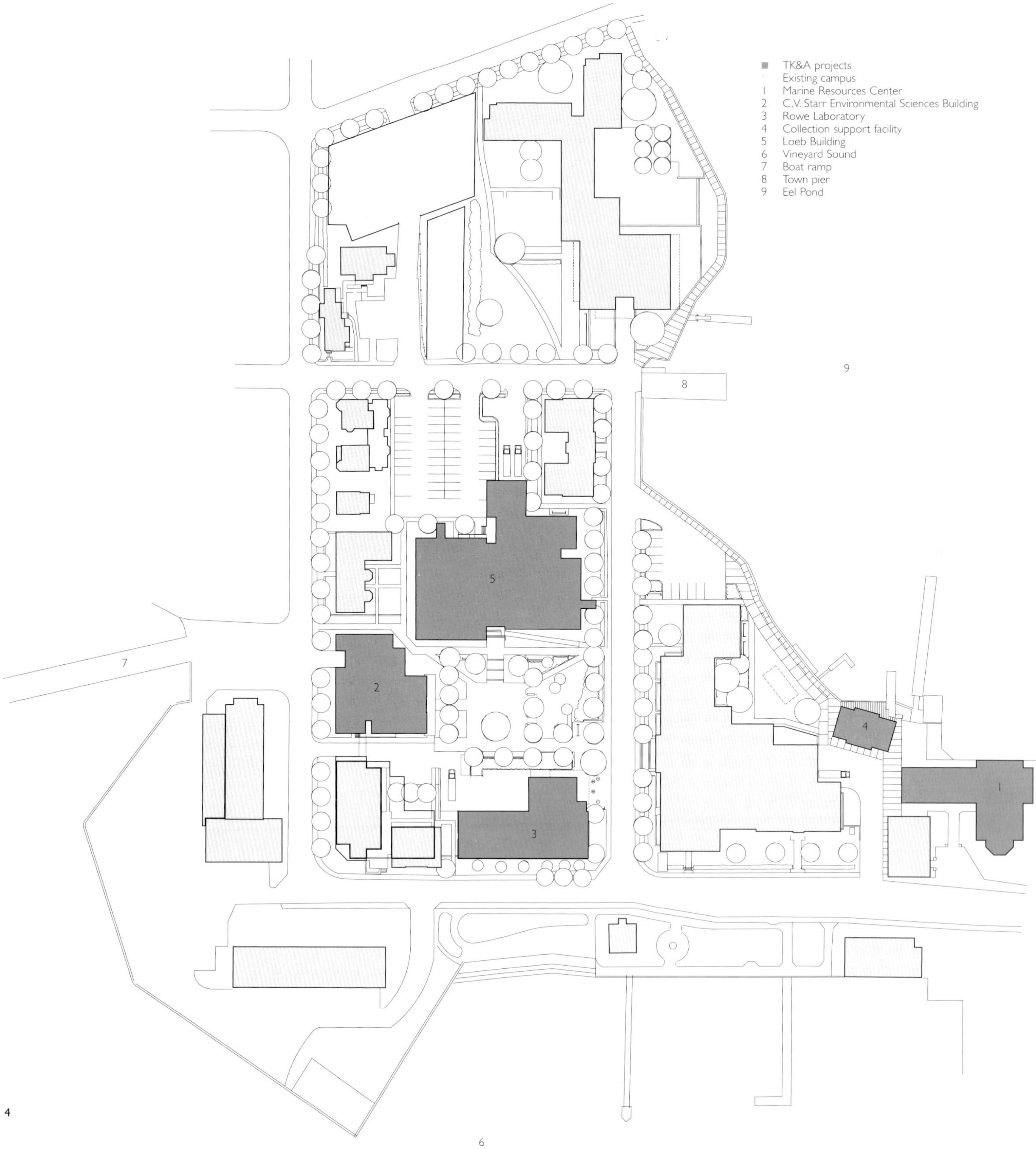
■ TK&A projects
Existing campus
1 Marine Resources Center
2 C.V. Starr Environmental Sciences Building
3 Rowe Laboratory
4 Collection support facility
5 Loeb Building
6 Vineyard Sound
7 Boat ramp
8 Town pier
9 Eel Pond
9
8
5
7
2
4
1
3
6

4

5

4 Site plan
5 Marine Resources Center aerial
6 Starr Building

6

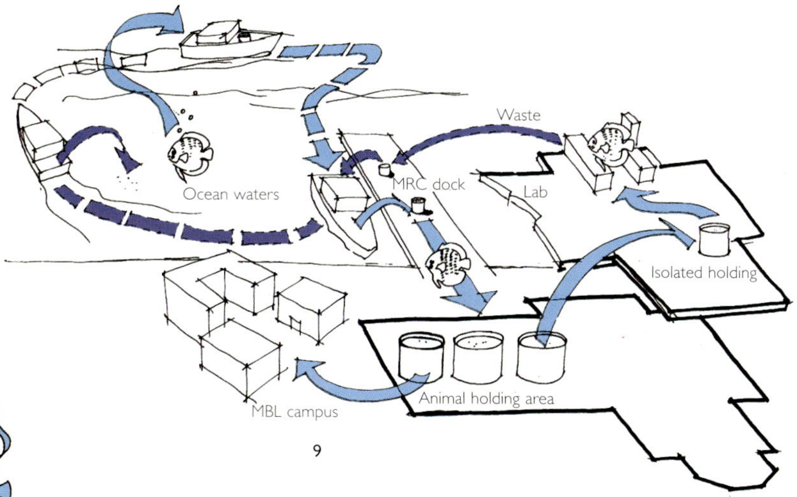

9

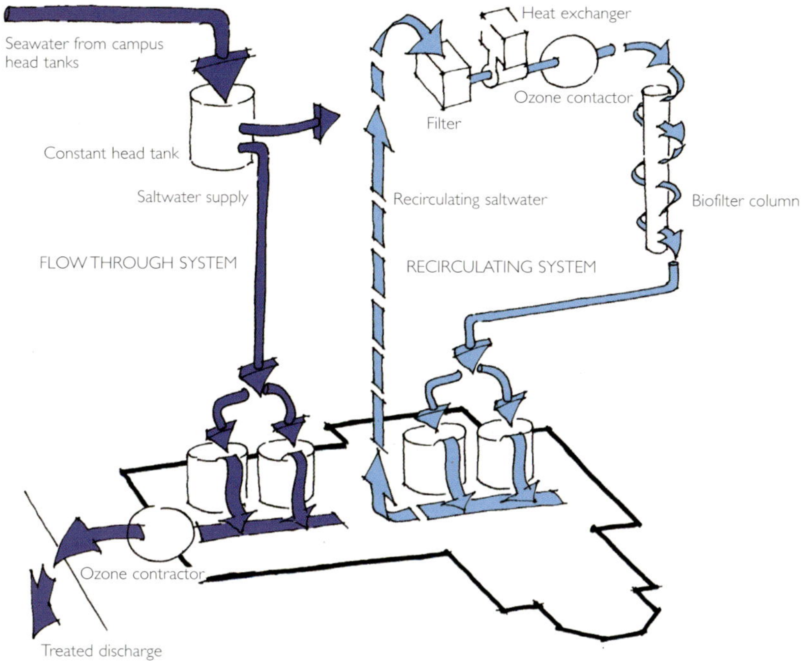

8

Opposite:
Rowe Building lobby
8 Life support
9 Materials handling
10 Marine Resources Center saltwater storage tanks
11 Rowe Building laboratory

10

11

tango

Location	Boston, Massachusetts
Completion	2005
Size	450,000 square feet

Opposite:
Street level
2 View from Cambridge Street

Davis Marcus Partners
Charles River Plaza

2

This redevelopment project transforms an underutilized 1960s-era mall and medical office building without pedestrian activity or street presence into a vibrant mixed-use complex that is well linked to its surrounding neighborhoods, Boston's historic Beacon Hill, and Government Center.

The project comprises two buildings that bring human scale and definition to one of the city's oldest streets while providing much-needed laboratory, research and development, office, and retail space.

The four-story building that fronts Cambridge Street serves as the complex's signature building. Filled with retail and restaurant tenants on the street level, the building attracts people to the area throughout the day and into the evening. The building's massing and height mask the second, eight-story building, which is set back from the street.

The taller building, the Richard B. Simches Research Center, is an interdisciplinary medical research facility occupied by Massachusetts General Hospital. The Simches Center is home to four cutting-edge disciplines that include genetic research and systems biology. The facility allows Mass General to expand its world-class research adjacent to its main campus, making the most of integrated resources and shared knowledge. The use of precast concrete, curtainwall, and aluminum allows the façade to blend into the densely developed urban cityscape while its gentle bow creates a view corridor that connects it to the surrounding residential neighborhood.

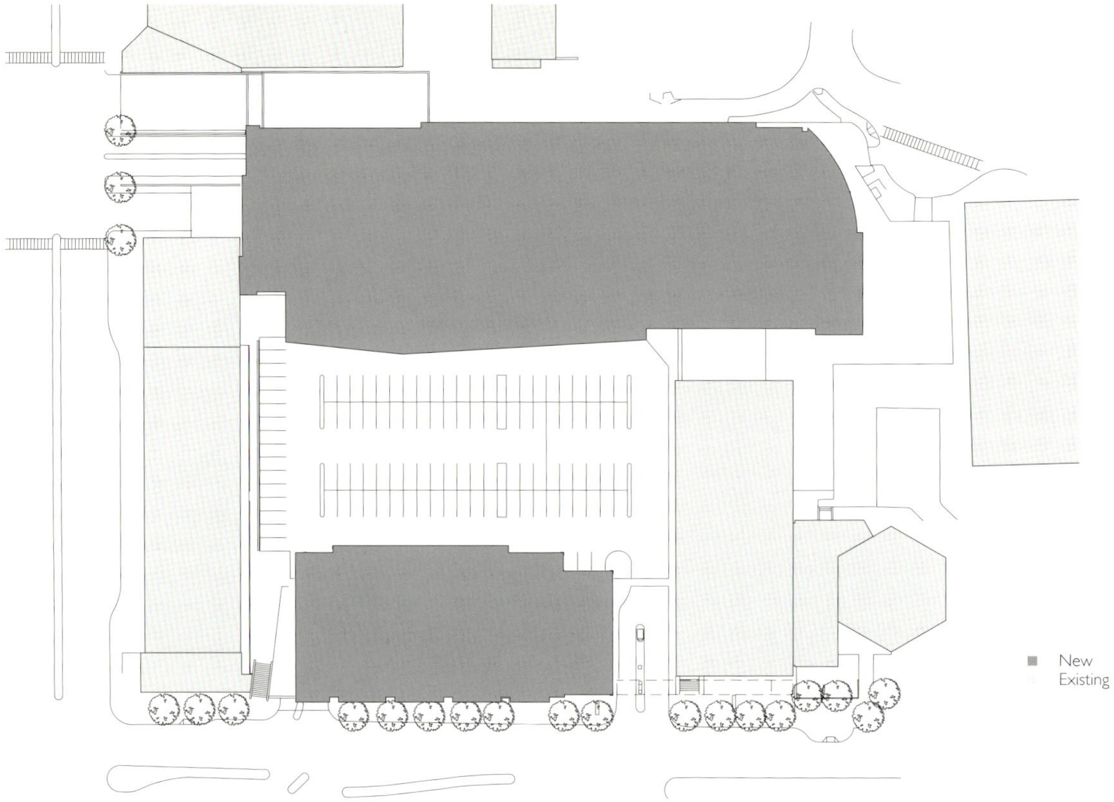

3

4

3 Site plan
4 Aerial
5 North-south section
6 East-west section
7 Façade detail

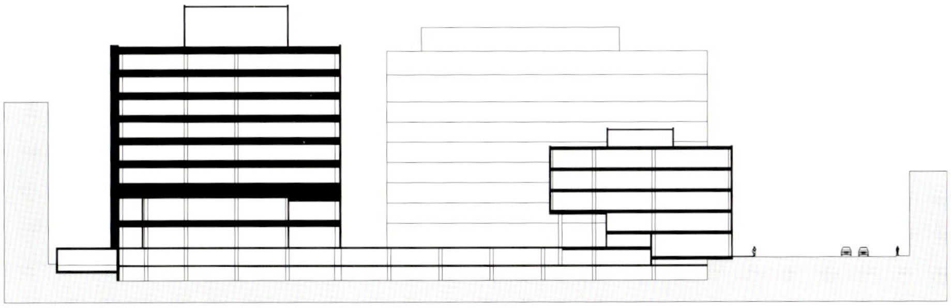

5

6

7

1

Location	Cambridge, Massachusetts
Completion	1999
Size	200,000 square feet

Forest City Enterprises | Millennium Pharmaceuticals

University Park at MIT

1 Entry canopy
2 View from park

2

A joint venture between the Massachusetts Institute of Technology and Forest City Enterprises, this university research park is one of the first to provide a complete mixed-use environment with laboratories, offices, housing, retail, and parking. The project involves the design of two research buildings as well as the fit-out for Millennium Pharmaceuticals' headquarters and R&D facilities, which occupies all of one building and part of the second.

The project employs a campus design solution rather than a signature, stand-alone approach. The buildings help to frame the park, which is at the center of the development's master plan. Two multilevel, glass-walled drums project from the building to announce its main entrances and offer open-air terraces where building users can enjoy views of the nearby urban cityscape. A bridge connects the buildings and creates a gateway from the park to the area's surrounding residential neighborhoods.

Millennium's facilities communicate the company's leading-edge image, transform its office culture from closed, private offices to open, flexible workspaces, and promote collaboration among staff and scientists across a variety of disciplines. Biology and chemistry laboratories, where researchers work most intensely, are located on the window wall. Non-lab workspaces are positioned away from the labs in an open-plan configuration that encourages interaction among fellow researchers.

Two multistory atria link the lab floors, connecting them visually and providing community gathering spaces. Common functions such as conference rooms are located off the atria on all floors. A large cafeteria doubles as a meeting space, and a seminar room is provided for scientific conferences. Each floor contains break rooms and additional public space to encourage informal interaction.

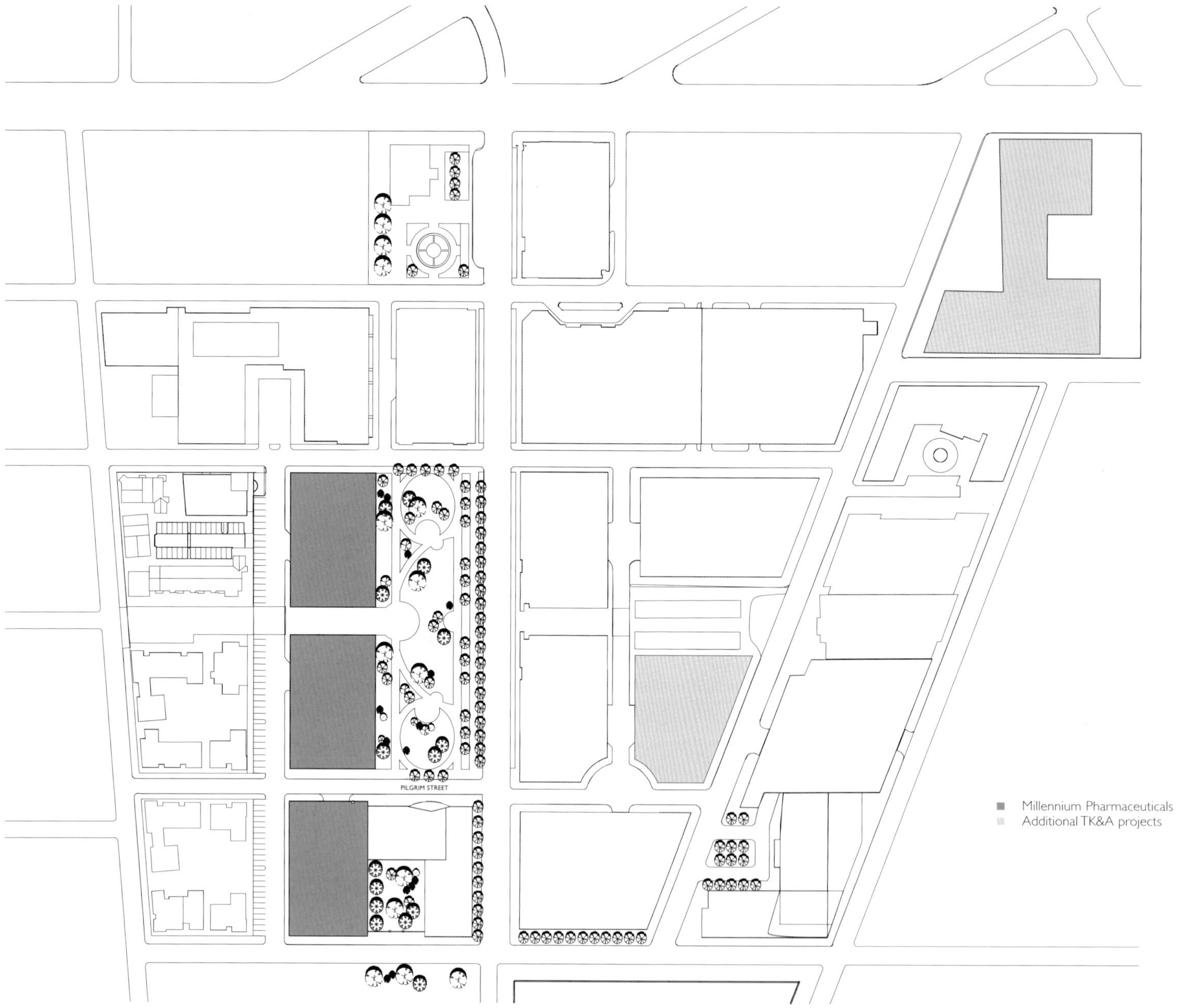

3

3 Campus plan
Opposite:
Entry drum

EXIT

Opposite:
Atrium stair
6 Internal lobby

6

I

Location	Boston, Massachusetts
Completion	1991
Size	122,000 square feet

1 View from Harvard Medical School
2 View from Longwood Avenue

Brigham and Women's Hospital
Eugene Braunwald Research Center

2

The six-story Eugene Braunwald Research Center is sited in one of the most densely developed research super blocks in the nation, Boston's Longwood Medical Area. The facility is part of a master plan for Brigham and Women's Hospital to meet the changing needs of biomedical investigators affiliated with Brigham and Women's Hospital and Harvard Medical School.

The Boston Lying-In Hospital, one of the United States' first maternity hospitals and an award-winning example of Bernini-style palazzo architecture, was razed to make way for the Eugene Braunwald Research Center. In consideration of that historical precedent and of nearby Harvard Medical School and its architecturally significant quadrangle, the new building controls its scale and develops an aesthetic that preserves and honors its varied urban influences without being imitative. The facility maintains the existing roofline and creates a fully integrated physical experience by employing a flat-plate concrete structural system to align its floors to those of neighboring buildings.

Setting a new standard for research space on the Brigham and Women's campus, the facility establishes a floor zoning system that is flexible and efficient while providing welcoming interior spaces for staff, investigators, administrators, and visitors. Labs, offices, and support areas are located consistently throughout each floor plate, with labs and support areas running parallel along the length of the corridors and offices clustered at the ends. This clustering achieves optimal cost efficiency and draws light into the core of the building.

The building represents the first implementation of the Harvard Medical School research module in an affiliated institution, a highly scalable model that is widely used throughout the United States today. Designed as a series of generically appointed modules, the labs can easily be customized, expanded, scaled back, and retrofitted in order to keep pace with the requirements of science. Equipment zones and support areas, including glass wash, procedure rooms, and cold rooms are shared by all tenants and are vertically stacked throughout the building to share systems components. Ceilings are exposed to increase the volume of the spaces, and ample storage systems are provided in support areas to keep corridors free for staff transit.

3

4

5

3 Elevator lobby
4 Laboratory
5 Stair detail

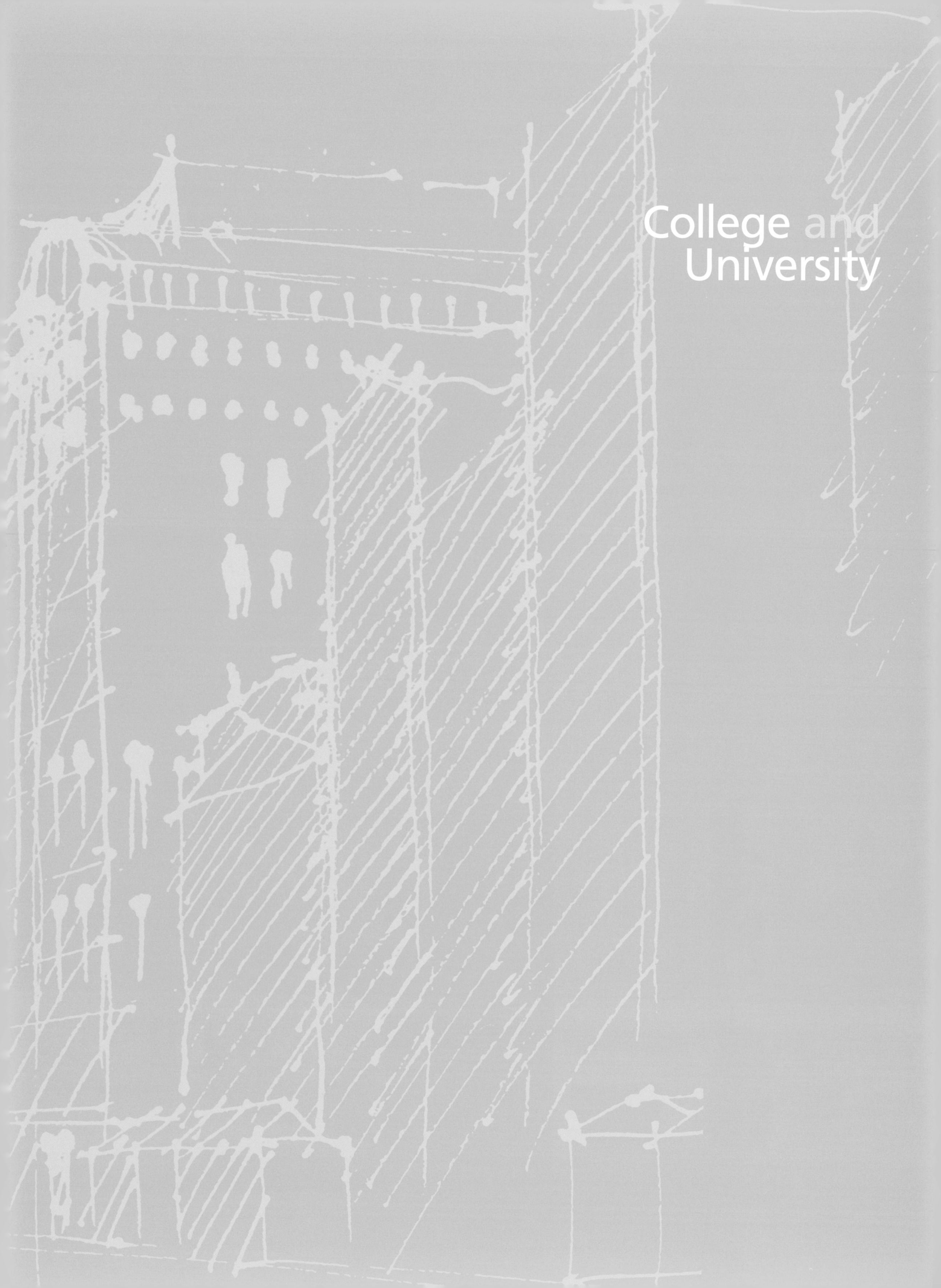

College and University

Location	Worcester, Massachusetts
Completion	2004
Size	50,000 square feet

Opposite:
View from neighborhood
2 Interaction space
3 View from quadrangle

Clark University
Lasry Center for Bioscience

2

3

This teaching and laboratory facility is the centerpiece of a new science quadrangle that expands, provides for future growth, and creates a distinct image for this traditional urban campus. The building puts the sciences on display and conveys Clark University's forward-looking mission while integrating into the campus fabric and surrounding neighborhood.

The building's exterior draws on a variety of existing campus elements and materials. Masonry cladding and a glazed curtainwall system were chosen with consideration for context, functional expression, and neighborhood scale.

The interior is organized around a three-story, skylit atrium that welcomes visitors to teaching and research labs, classrooms, seminar rooms, faculty offices, lounges, and "chalk-talk" areas. Light and transparency animate and expand the interior, promoting collegiality and projecting warmth and comfort. Delineated alcoves and other intimate spaces provide opportunities for private study and reflection. Brick, glass, wood, terrazzo, and other time-honored materials and finishes lend the building an air of distinction and refinement.

The Lasry Center is the eighth facility in Massachusetts to achieve LEED gold certification from the U.S. Green Building Council. Sustainable design principles were observed from the project's inception, beginning with a site selection process that considered solar orientation, tree preservation opportunities, and impervious area reduction. The building is 45 percent more energy-efficient and uses 30 percent less water than the average laboratory building its size, and its trianglular shape allows the building to achieve maximum southern exposure throughout. Aluminum shades over windows on the western and southern façades deflect sun and heat from the interior during warmer months and reflect heat indoors in the winter.

4 Site plan
5 Façade detail
6 Lounge
Opposite:
Atrium

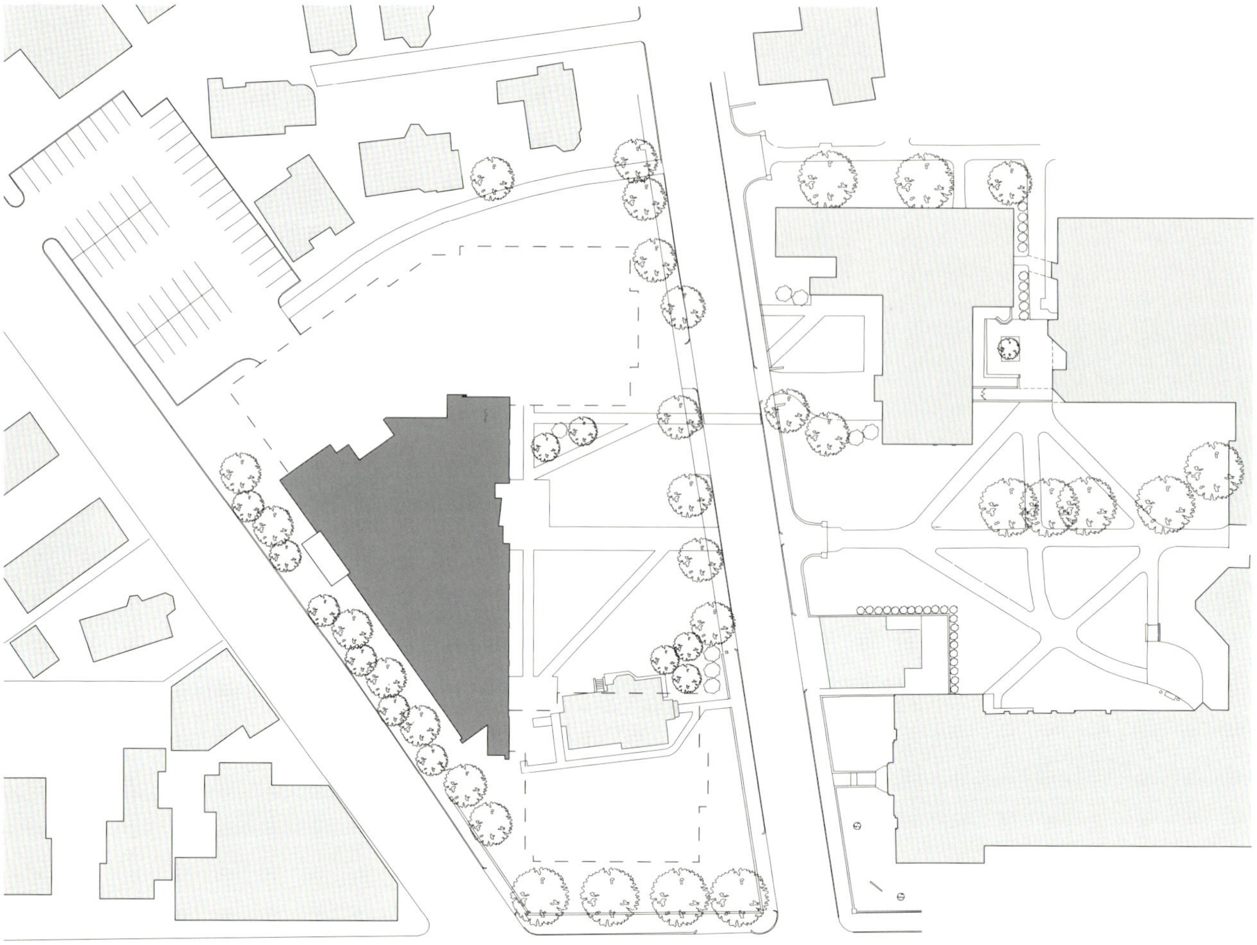

4

5

6

Location	St. Louis, Missouri
Completion	2004
Size	151,180 square feet

Opposite:
East entrance
2 Main entry

Washington University in St. Louis
Earth and Planetary Sciences Building

2

The Earth and Planetary Sciences Building at Washington University in St. Louis provides a single facility suited to the teaching and research activities of one of the country's few academic programs to make direct use of knowledge gained by exploring the solar system. Among the department's research activities are several NASA programs associated with the Viking Lander and Mars Exploration Rover.

The building strengthens the Collegiate Gothic character of the campus. By employing an asymmetric arrangement of building elements and using local stone materials in the vernacular style, it introduces a contemporary, human scale to its mass and courtyard spaces. Providing the department with a strong physical identity, the building also is consistent with the original Cope & Stewardson campus plan.

Innovative mechanical systems help resolve the dichotomy between Collegiate Gothic design principals—including short walls and gabled roofs—and the technical demands of a state-of-the-art teaching and research facility. A localized fan coil system reduces the need for outside air ventilation while exposed ductwork offers visual relief to the low floor-to-floor heights and lends an air of openness. To accommodate the building's extensive mechanical equipment, exhaust towers are concealed within chimneys, and cooling towers and exhaust fans are placed in roof wells.

The clustering of research disciplines in the building's discreet wings fosters collaboration among researchers and allows for greater operational efficiencies. Lounge spaces, conference rooms, and shared teaching spaces encourage interaction among students, faculty, and visitors. On the lower level, an earth sciences museum encourages public traffic while the library and study areas are located in more private spaces on the second floor.

Reflecting the Earth-focused nature of the research it supports, the building is designed with consideration of its impact on natural resources. It achieved LEED silver certification from the U.S. Green Building Council.

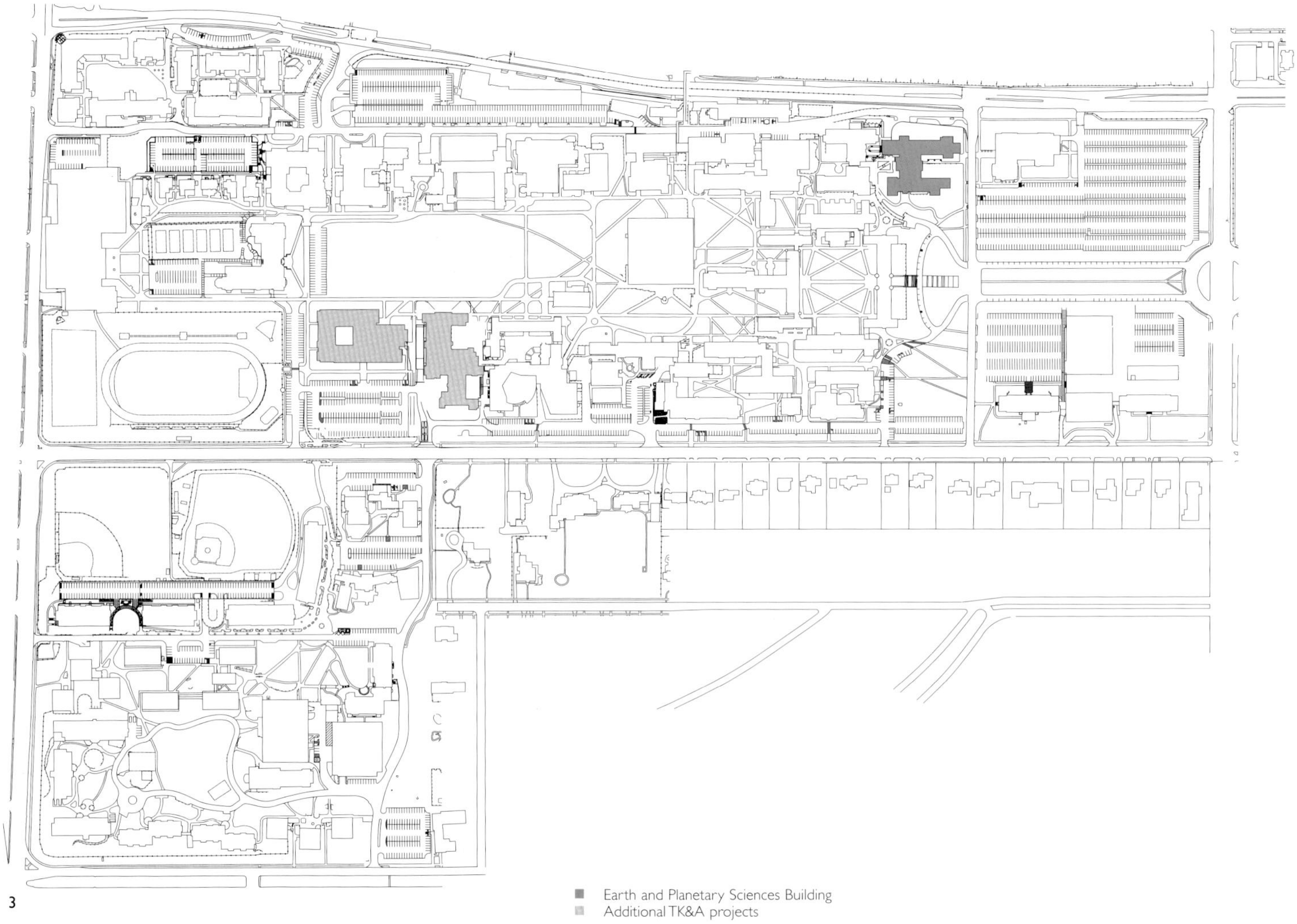

3

Earth and Planetary Sciences Building
Additional TK&A projects

3 Site plan
4 Concept sketch
5 South entrance

4

5

6

6 Library
7 Break room

7

Location	Cambridge, Massachusetts
Completion	2004
Size	38,000 square feet

Opposite:
Patio
2 Café seating

Harvard Law School
Harkness Commons

2

One of eight buildings designed by Walter Gropius in 1949, Harkness Commons is among Cambridge's most important examples of American Modern architecture. Originally intended to house graduate students, the building evolved into a student center and over time was portioned into multiple awkward spaces. This renovation restores and repairs the building's exterior while modernizing and improving the functionality of its interior spaces.

Columns and brickwork are repaired and the original limestone façade, now patched and cleaned, is restored to a rich patina. Low-E insulating glass and thermally broken aluminum frames with matching mullion widths maintain the visual profile of the original windows while providing contemporary efficiencies.

At street level, a new patio with a seating area reinforces the building's connection to the adjacent quadrangle while providing access to the law school campus. To promote outside life and collegiality during long New England winters, a portion of the facility's lawn can be flooded to encourage ice-skating.

The reconfigured interior makes optimal use of the building's expansive curve and the abundant natural light that had been almost completely blocked during previous renovations. On the ground floor, a newly open study area features a historic working fireplace designed by Joseph Albers that was uncovered during renovation. The main concourse, previously a dark tunnel of granite paving stone, now provides a bright and welcoming thoroughfare. The main dining room on the second floor, restored to a single expansive space, opens up views to the quadrangle and offers glimpses of the student life within to curious passersby.

Several pieces of distinguished artwork that have long contributed to the building's Bauhaus aesthetic are preserved in this renovation. Joan Miró's ceramic replica of an oil painting, originally hung in 1950, hangs in the dining room while a Herbert Bayer glass screen wall graces the head of the stairs. Bayer's mosaic tile wall on the east side of the ramp is covered with removable fabric-wrapped panels to lighten the space without damaging the artwork.

3 Original Gropius exterior
4 Site plan
5 Dining room
6 Level one floor plan
7 Level two floor plan

3

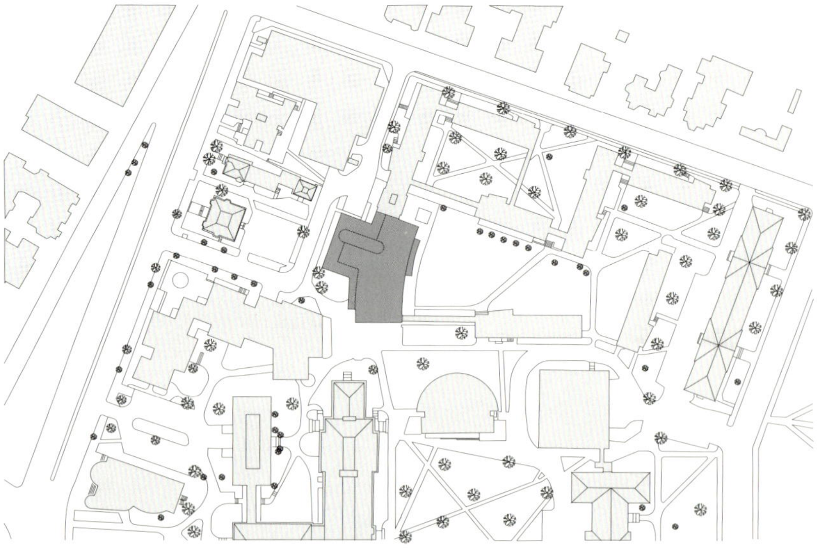

4

5

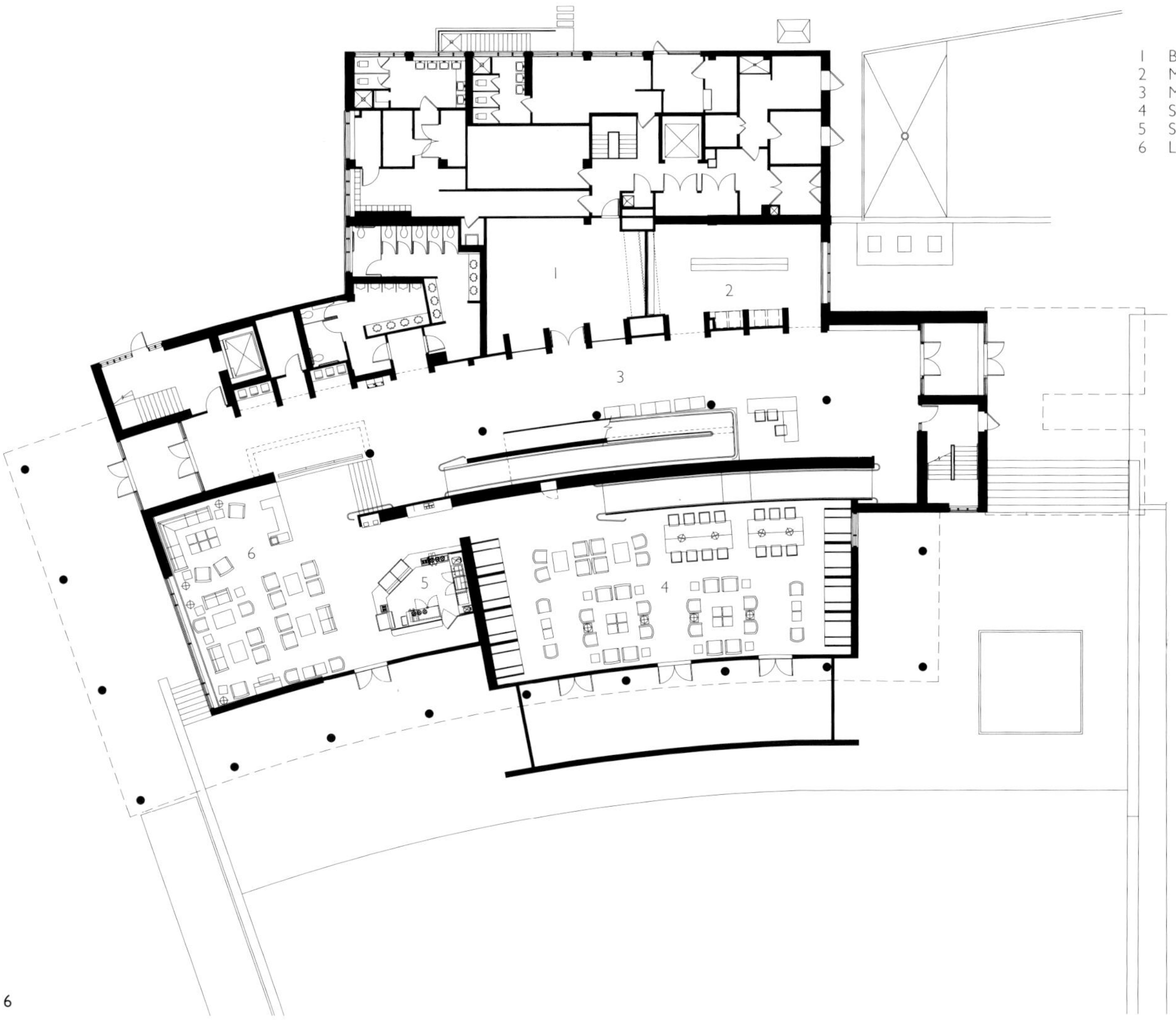
1 Bookstore
2 Mailroom
3 Main concourse
4 Study area
5 Snack bar
6 Lounge

6

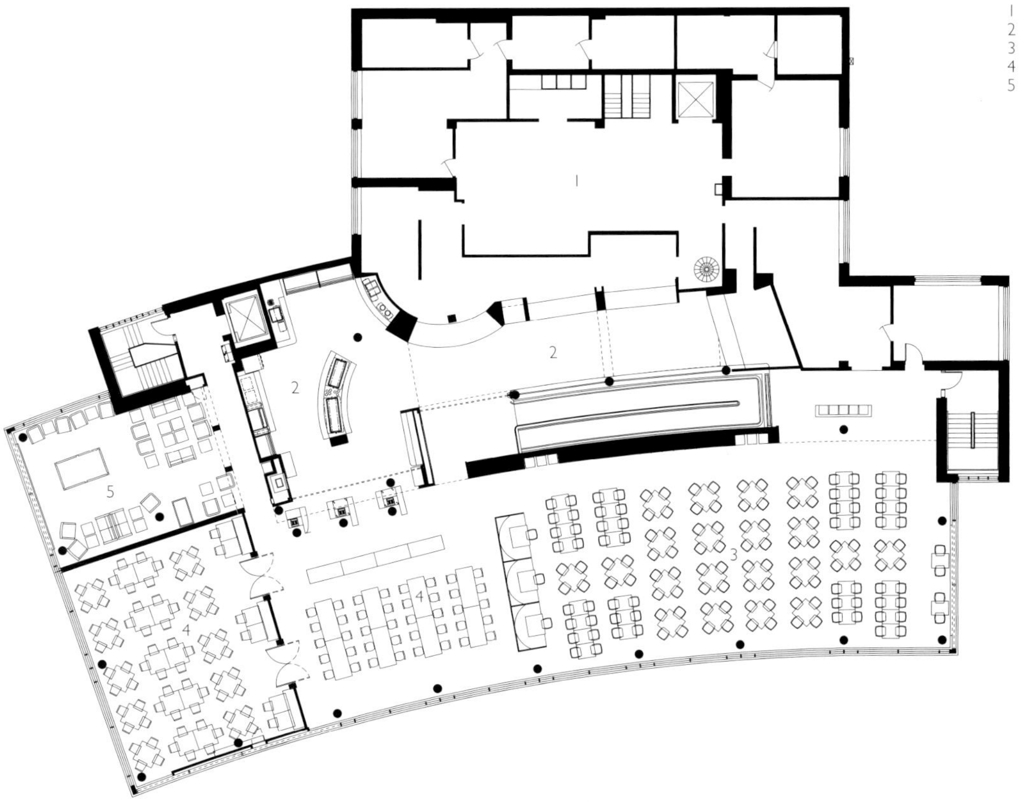
1 Main kitchen
2 Servery
3 Dining room
4 Café
5 Pub

7

FRIED
DOUGH
JOBS FOR YOUTH

Location	Boston, Massachusetts
Completion	1999
Size	293,000 square feet

Opposite:
View from Boston Common
2 Tremont Street entry

Suffolk University Law School

David J. Sargent Hall

2

Located on one of Boston's most prominent sites, Sargent Hall brings a distinguished physical identity to the nation's third-largest law school and adds a contemporary architectural statement to an area of Boston that is steeped in history. The building centralizes Suffolk University Law School and enhances its role as a community leader and resource while elevating the proud tradition of the study of law.

The building's symmetrical entry façade is dignified but not monumental and plays against its simple massing. The sidewalk widens to give the building a special presence on the street and a subtle bow announces the entry portico. Indiana limestone, granite, and stainless steel blend comfortably and elegantly with the surrounding neighborhood, and large areas of curtainwall glass act as counterpoints to massive walls.

The interior is made up of a four-story space connected by an atrium known as the Great Hall and a three-story space dedicated to library users that is also connected by an atrium and stairs. The stacked atria organize the space and create a vertical campus that encourages interaction among the law school community and supports public activities.

Key interior elements include tri-colored French limestone on the main floor of the Great Hall, stately columns that echo the entrance portico, and an oculus at the apex of the Great Hall that reveals a colorful fabric dome. At the building's top levels, the law library offers spectacular natural light and city views. Renewable wood and other rich materials and finishes are incorporated throughout the facility to create refined and timeless environments.

Eighteen classrooms range in size from seminar rooms that hold 24 people to lecture halls that accommodate 130. All classrooms as well as the three moot court rooms and the library feature the most advanced, flexible data and audiovisual capabilities. This commitment to technology, together with the facilities provided by this premier new building, has enhanced Suffolk's local and national reputation and boosted morale among students and faculty.

3 Roofscapes
4 Entry elevation
5&6 Concept sketches
Following pages:
View from historic Granary Burial Ground

3

4

5

6

ONE WAY

8

9

10

1 Entry lobby
2 Great Hall
3 Advanced legal studies
4 Career services
5 Registrar
6 Financial Aid
7 Admissions
8 Development
9 Function room
10 Clinical programs
11 Student lockers
12 Bookstore
13 Mail room
14 Parking garage entrance
15 Loading dock

11

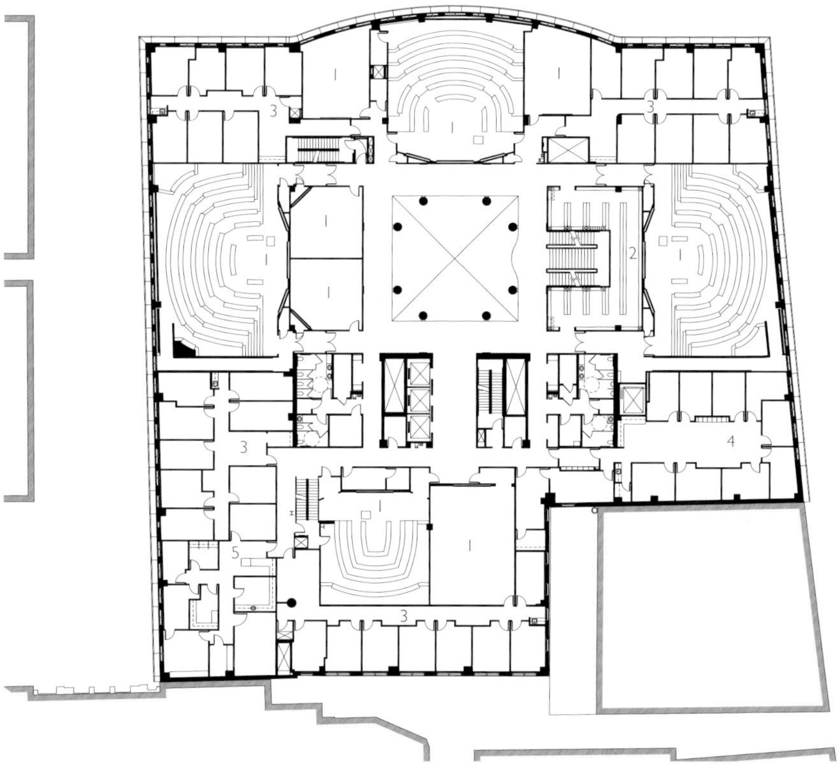

1 Classrooms
2 Student lockers
3 Faculty offices
4 Legal practice skills
5 Media services

12

8 Great Hall
9 Main reading room
10 Commons
11 Entry level floor plan
12 Level two floor plan

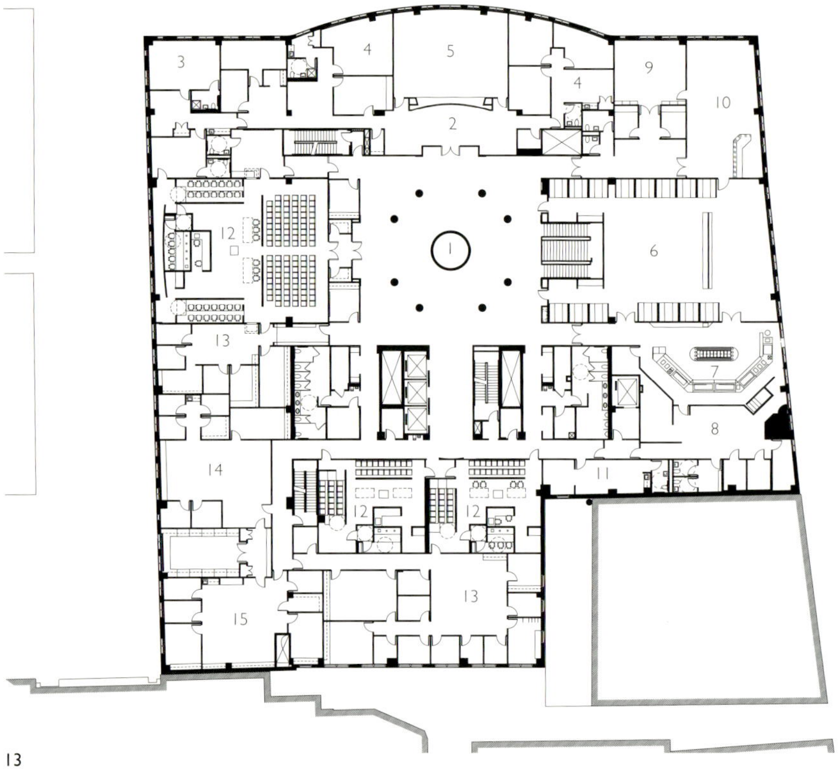

1 The Commons
2 Reception
3 President's office
4 Deans' offices
5 Faculty meeting room
6 Cafeteria
7 Servery
8 Kitchen
9 Alumni lounge
10 Faculty dining
11 Lounge
12 Moot court rooms
13 Student organizations
14 Law review
15 Transitional law review

13

14

13 Level six floor plan
14 Moot court room
15 East-west section
16 Electronic classroom

1 Great Hall
2 Classrooms
3 Offices
4 Student office
5 Student organizations
6 Moot court room
7 Study carrels
8 Small group studies
9 Deans' offices
10 Terminal/printer room
11 Reception
12 Lounge
13 Small group studies
14 Main reading room
15 Reading room
16 The Commons
17 Conference room
18 Parking garage
19 Pre-function space
20 Function room

15

16

Location	Philadelphia, Pennsylvania
Completion	2004
Size	128,000 square feet

Opposite:
Stair
2 Street view

Following pages:
3 Atrium
4 Corridor
5 Lobby
Opposite:
Entry

University of Pennsylvania School of Medicine | Forest City Enterprises

Translational Research Center

2

Located on the northeast edge of the University of Pennsylvania's campus, this renovation and addition transforms a contaminated and neglected historic industrial building once used for manufacturing transformers into a state-of-the-art wet lab facility. Developed as part of the Penn master campus plan, the project joins a burgeoning neighborhood of research, academic, housing, street-level retail, commercial, and recreational facilities.

Private developer Forest City Enterprises partnered with Penn to share construction risks and to expedite the design and construction process, a collaboration that freed Penn to concentrate on its core research mission. The facility was launched within 22 months, alleviating Penn's immediate need for flexible and efficient laboratory space to support its School of Medicine.

Upgraded to improve its appearance and energy efficiency, the building envelope incorporates large two-story insulated windows, and a new entrance was added. The interior spaces are flooded with natural light that pours through the central portion of the roof, now opened to include a linear skylight along the building's spine.

Labs and related offices are concentrated on the second floor and on the west end of the first floor where daylight is plentiful. Heavier, service-oriented functions are located proximally to the loading dock on the east end of the first floor. The building's chief circulation occurs along the center of its spine, allowing incidental and informal interaction among researchers before they venture north or south into modular labs outfitted for their particular specialty.

The building layout is easily adapted to a variety of research styles and functions, a strategy that provides flexibility for evolving science. Multiple lab benches built on a standard dimensional module allow for easy research team or departmental space assignments. Customizable lab support areas are provided for scientific, environmental, or safety controls. Desks for lab technicians are located adjacent to the lab benches, generally near exterior windows or under clerestory windows on the central spine where researchers work in natural daylight and have access to views of the nearby urban cityscape. Office and meeting rooms are also clustered near exterior walls or on the spine to take advantage of natural light and a visual connection to the outdoors.

3

4

5

125

1 Quadrangle view
2 Lobby
3 Conference room

1

Location	Boston, Massachusetts
Completion	1985-1993
Size	862,800 square feet

Harvard Medical School
Quadrangle Renovations

2

3

The five buildings that flank the Harvard Medical School quadrangle, which was constructed in 1912, hold significant historical value for the school and play a major role in defining its architectural heritage. The master plan called for modernizing four of the buildings to bring the school's medical, academic, and research missions into the 21st century while continuing to honor the intentions of the quadrangle's original architect.

A portion of Building A's interior, including the dean's office, was preserved in its original form but the atrium area on the top three floors of the five-story structure was completely refurbished, creating new administrative offices, conference rooms, faculty and alumni meeting areas, and the computer center.

The Countway Library gained a new dean's boardroom that overlooks the entire quadrangle from a fifth-floor corner. A custom-built armoire divides the room, which can now be used for both small luncheons and large meetings.

Four U-shaped buildings housed the medical school's Basic Science departments. Building C, home to antiquated laboratory and research space for the Department of Biological Chemistry and Molecular Pharmacology, was completely gutted, leaving only its marble Neoclassical shell. The five-story building's two wings now house modern biochemistry and physiology laboratories that flank a 120-seat auditorium. Light maple walls and brightly colored finishes and accents throughout the public spaces present a warm counterpoint to the clinical appearance of the laboratories. Custom variable-volume fume hoods with airflow controls were used in the laboratories to respond to lower-than-average floor-to-floor heights. A non-conventional service strategy introduces vertical stacks for shared systems to achieve a high degree of energy efficiency.

By adding an entire floor atop the existing neoclassical building, Building D is expanded to house both new and refurbished research laboratory space for the departments of Pathology and Microbiology. The additional floor's façade is rendered in modern Terne-coated stainless steel to resemble its historical counterpart. The addition preserves the silhouette of the white marble façade while complementing the original composition. As Buildings C and D were originally designed for laboratories, their bay size is suitable for contemporary lab modules. To achieve contemporary efficiencies while planning for future growth and change, however, a modular approach was used in designing the floor layouts.

Planning for new facilities, including the Warren Alpert Building and the Harvard Institutes of Medicine, allowed for staged implementation as required by program growth. Also planned was a below-grade parking structure, to be covered by a restored Harvard Medical School quadrangle, a historic part of Olmstead's Emerald Necklace at the terminus of Avenue Louis Pasteur.

4 Site plan
5 Auditorium
Opposite:
Stair

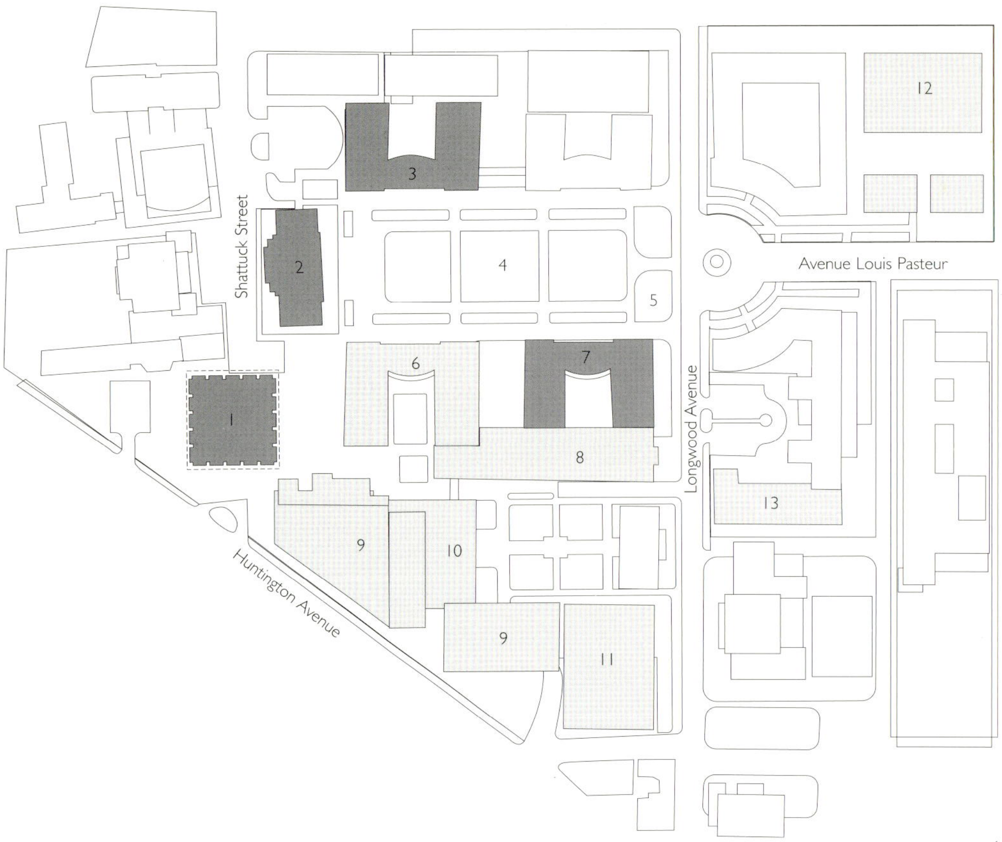

■ Quadrangle renovations
Additional TK&A projects and studies

1 Countway Library
2 Building A
3 Building C
4 Harvard Medical School quadrangle
5 Parking under quadrangle
6 Building B
7 Building D
8 Warren Alpert Building
9 School of Public Health
10 Proposed School of Public Health addition
11 School of Dental Medicine, future expansion
12 Harvard Institutes of Medicine
13 Eugene Braunwald Research Center

4

5

2

Opposite:
Atrium
8 Laboratory
9 Boardroom

8

9

General Practice

Location	Boston, Massachusetts
Completion	2002
Size	135,000 square feet

Opposite:
Façade detail
2 City view

Intercontinental Developers
Nine Zero Hotel

2

This four-star boutique hotel soars 19 stories above some of Boston's most historic sites and buildings, offering coveted views of the dense urban cityscape. The hotel houses 190 guest rooms plus office suites, fitness facilities, a signature bar, and a restaurant.

The building's location on a prominent corner site near Boston Common required a careful consideration of context and scale. By combining exterior materials such as classic brick and limestone with contemporary glass curtainwall and steel, the building integrates with its historic context while putting a modern twist on the existing architectural traditions and aesthetic of the neighborhood.

The proportional elements of the composition were based on the Chicago-style high-rise brick buildings of Louis Sullivan, drawing the eye upward with clean lines that emphasize the hotel's vertical rise. The large expanse of glass on the upper floors reads like the top of a lighthouse, allowing the building to be viewed as a beacon from afar. Closer up, the hotel has a more intimate feel. Generous public spaces along the street edge preserve the pedestrian scale and character of the neighborhood. Large windows offer views into the building for passersby and views out to nearby historic landmarks for the guests inside.

A low floor-to-floor height is achieved by stacking all utilities to run vertically through cast-in-place concrete slabs with designated chases cut in each. This particular economy allows for the addition of another guest floor while still keeping the building within the city's fixed-height zoning limit of 175 feet. The building achieved the then-highest project floor area ratio in the City of Boston and enjoys a highly efficient design that maximizes the revenue-generating capacity of the site.

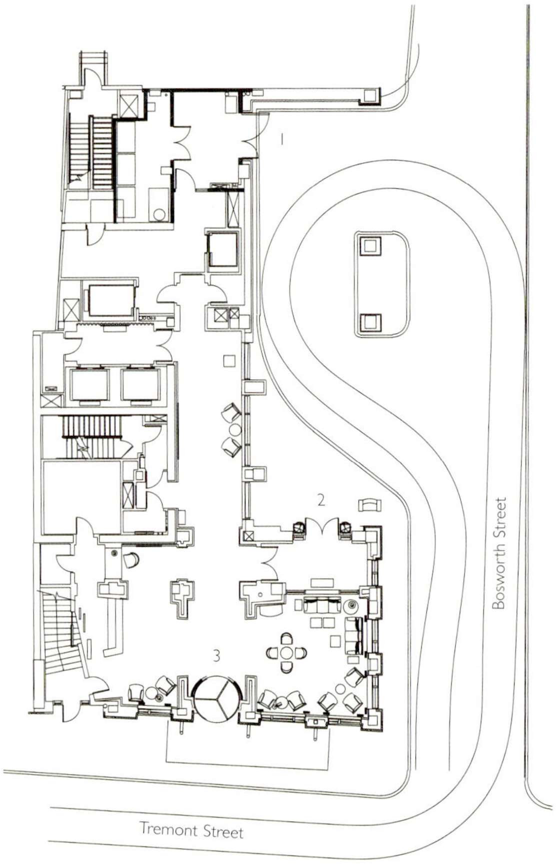

1 Receiving
2 Entry court
3 Lobby

3

4

5

3 Site plan
4 Typical floor plan
5 Entry canopy
6 View from Boston Common

6

1 Courtyard
2 Entry canopy
Following pages:
Entry façade

1

Location	Needham, Massachusetts
Completion	2001
Size	400,000 square feet

Parametric Technology Corporation | Boston Properties

Corporate Headquarters

2

The Parametric Technology Corporation headquarters complex transforms a former brownfield site in a 1960s-era industrial park into a vibrant, campus-like setting that celebrates the surrounding public conservation land while creating a human-scaled environment that prioritizes pedestrians and open spaces over automobile traffic. Located on the partial beltway outside of Boston dubbed "America's Technology Highway," the facility employs responsible principles of smart growth and reflects a new model for dense suburban redevelopment.

The main entrance, a glass-enclosed pavilion that overlooks an abutting pond, includes a dining facility for employees and a visitor center for prospective clients. Gourmet catering, outdoor terraces, and a golf putting green make the pavilion a popular gathering place for executives and staff. Other amenities include a 10,000-square-foot fitness center and a customer collaboration and demonstration theater.

Bridges connect the four office buildings and a parking garage, providing all-weather access, intercommunication among departments, and flexibility for future growth. The facilities have allowed Parametric Technology Corporation to consolidate all of its operations, contributing to a more pronounced corporate identity, a surge in recruitment, improved customer relations, and increased productivity and efficiency. The redevelopment has also spurred the development of other projects nearby.

PTC

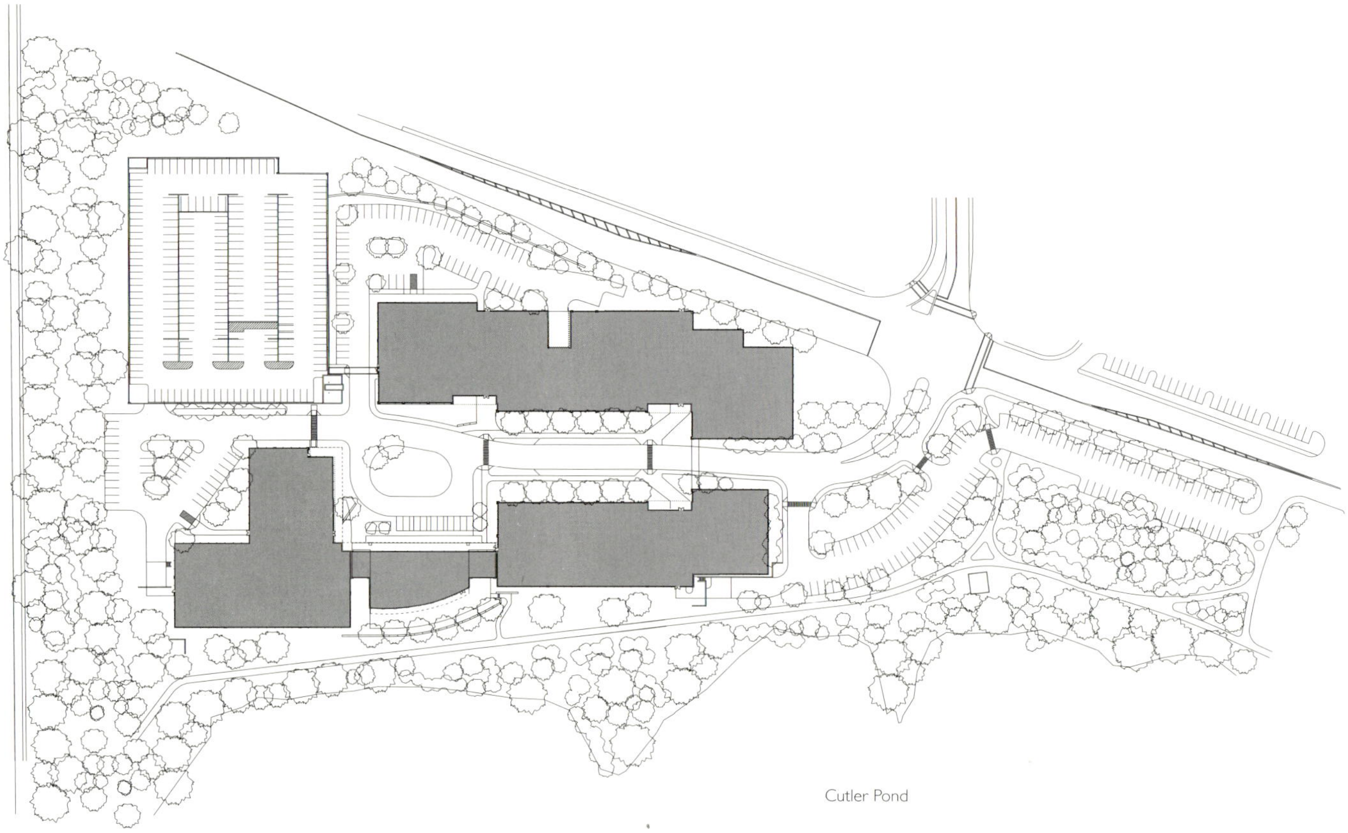

4

5

4 Site plan
5 Patio facing Cutler Pond
6 Campus model

6

1 Entry façade
2 Concept drawing

1

Location	Cambridge, Massachusetts
Completion	2000
Size	60,000 square feet

Intercontinental Developers

Winthrop Square

2

Revitalizing a previously neglected city block in historic Harvard Square, Winthrop Square is a mixed-use residential, office, and retail complex that includes two low-scale renovations of historically significant buildings, a new seven-story tower, and a single level of underground parking.

The new brick-and-limestone building affirms rather than tempers the traditional character of the neighborhood, offering simple massing and a strong fifth-floor cornice line to reduce its apparent scale. The building's sweeping curve provides a backdrop for the smaller historic buildings and the adjoining Colonial-era park that it faces while presenting narrow, townhouse-like façades at street level. Landscaped footpaths create a welcoming, easy-to-navigate way for pedestrians to travel the block, and a communal courtyard announces the entrances into Winthrop Square's residences.

One of Harvard Square's few remaining examples of a 19th-century wood-frame mansard duplex was preserved, refurbished, relocated, and reused for this project. The historic building was rotated 180 degrees and moved approximately 80 feet from its original location to achieve optimal adjacency to the park, to make the most of the site's maximum available square footage, and to facilitate construction of the below-grade parking.

1 Approach from Memorial Drive
2 View from Charles River

1

Location	Cambridge, Massachusetts
Completion	1994
Size	236,250 square feet

MIT Real Estate

640 Memorial Drive

2

This conversion of a 1913 Model T Ford factory brings biotechnology and high-technology laboratory and office space to the banks of the Charles River, leading a wave of redevelopment that serves and defines the highly visible scientific community at the Massachusetts Institute of Technology and Harvard University.

Long established as an urban landmark, the building's river-facing brick and white terracotta façade was carefully cleaned and restored using the original materials or exact replicas when possible, with the rest covered in fiberglass castings that match the color and finish. All of the riverside windows were replaced with insulated glass panels, though the small panes at the top carefully echo the original mullion pattern. Larger panes at the tenant levels offer unrestricted views of Boston while adding transparency to this historic contribution to the skyline.

Once a five-story train shed to which a metal lean-to structure was added, the north façade now presents Cambridge with a sun-filled, glass-enclosed, two-and-a-half-story lobby filled with warm, human-scaled details that make the space a welcome setting for casual collegial encounters. With 40,000-square-foot floor plates, the building offers maximum flexibility for dividing space, allowing for the facility's interior to be reconfigured to meet changing tenant's spatial requirements. The addition of two separate elevator cores increases this flexibility while decreasing the need for extensive interior corridors.

Details in the public space are rendered with natural materials and finishes to honor the earthy spirit of the building's industrial past while providing contemporary comfort and efficiency. A curved wall of Ash with highly visible grain brings warmth and texture to the building and acts as a counterpoint to the rigidity of its original design. The groove left after removing train tracks that once ran beneath the lobby now serves as a planter for an interior line of trees that connects tenants to the outdoors.

3

3 Entry
4 Atrium
5 Former Model T factory
6 Former train shed

4

5

6

Location	Cambridge, Massachusetts
Completion	1989
Size	265,000 square feet

Opposite:
View to Charles River
2 Entry

Lotus Development Corporation
Corporate Headquarters

2

Awarded as part of a design competition, this project represents one of the first built examples of the marriage between the academic community and private high-technology enterprise for which the Kendall Square area of Cambridge has since become internationally known. The goal of the project, which includes an office building and connected parking garage, was to provide a state-of-the-art facility that would advance the software development efforts of and attract top talent to Lotus, creator of the groundbreaking Lotus 1-2-3 spreadsheet application.

Reinforcing the building's connection to its East Cambridge neighborhood and its relationship to the nearby Charles River were primary design drivers. Creating open space on the site and links from the street to a future park was another goal, and the classic exterior design and materials allow the building to integrate seamlessly into its context. The modified U shape envelops a landscaped courtyard that acts as urban space and public thoroughfare and announces the building entrance. The shape also affords river views from every floor of the building.

A two-story atrium serves as the reception lobby/waiting area, providing views to the courtyard on one side and the river on the other and functioning also as an orientation point in the large building. A cafeteria, childcare center, sundries shop, and lecture hall stem from the lobby, and a curved central stairway leads to the second level.

Group work areas and offices are clustered as "neighborhoods," and gather along continuous curved corridors. A simple palette of materials throughout the building complements the architectural design and reflects the company's progressive, forward-looking image.

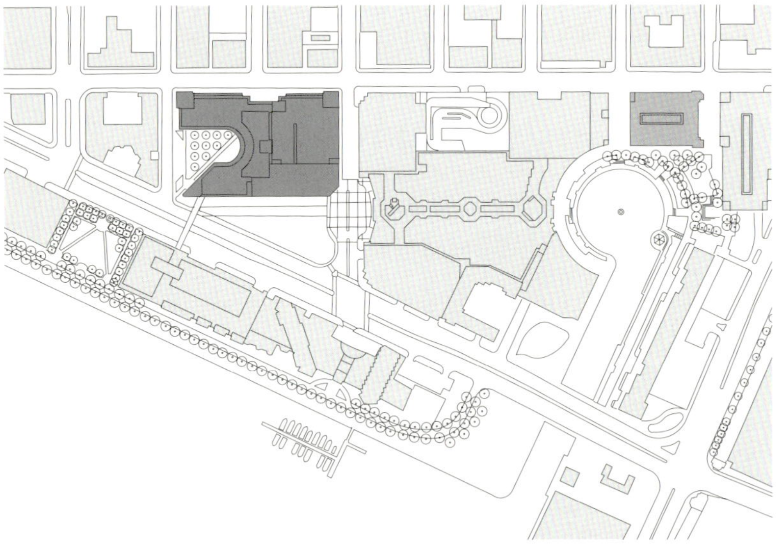

3

4

5

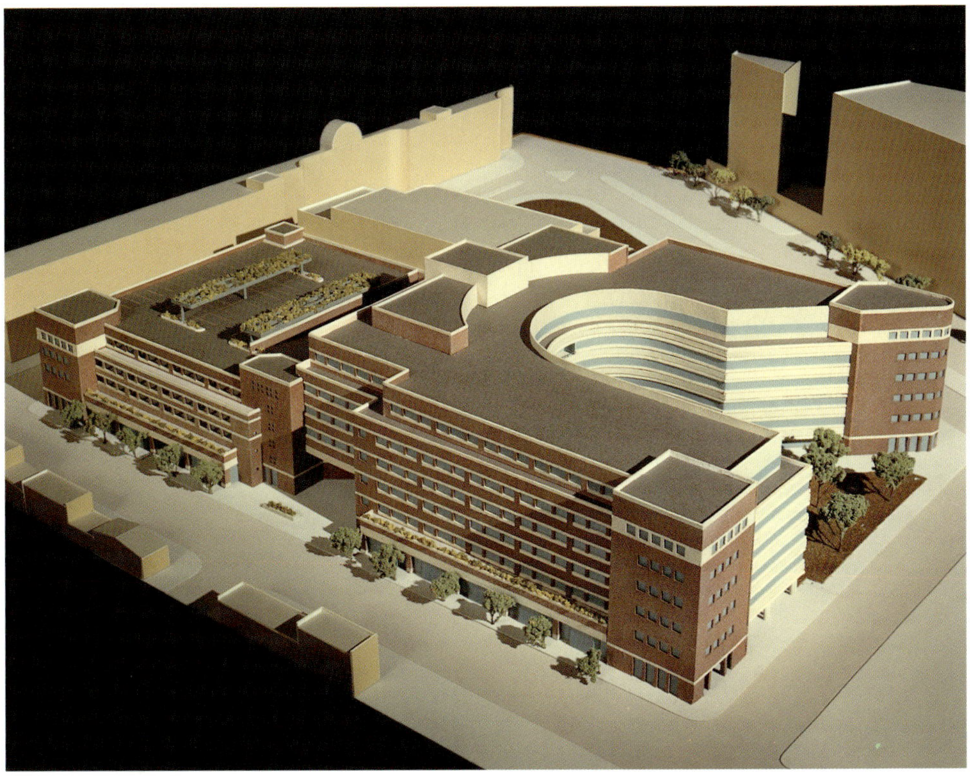

6

7

3 Site plan
4 View from Eliot Park
5 Courtyard
6 Campus model
7 Lobby

Planning

1

Location	Chapel Hill, North Carolina
Completion	2007
Size	4,000,000+ square feet

UNC Health Care and UNC-Chapel Hill School of Medicine

Master Plan

1 Hospital aerial
2 Patient Access Center approach

2

UNC Health Care and UNC-Chapel Hill School of Medicine plan to become the leading public academic health center in the country. This ambitious strategic goal requires a master plan that considers the legacy of the nation's oldest state university while remaining intently focused on creating a 21st-century physical environment that promotes collaboration among the clinical, education, and research missions on the Chapel Hill campus.

To determine a roadmap for development over the next 20 years, the master plan assessed the institutions' existing physical environment and infrastructure. Supporting this analysis was an evaluation of healthcare and research trends and their impact on future facility needs, and a determination of changes needed to help achieve key strategic goals.

The institutions are sited on 125 acres of contiguous ground known as the campus Health District. To improve access throughout the previously congested area, the master plan calls for the implementation of a spatial system to induce orderly automobile traffic, clear and efficient wayfinding, footpaths for pedestrians, and a unifying network of open spaces. It also delineates access points to nearby transportation and transit networks and the creation of convenient parking sites. Programming is blended between the best of the existing facilities and new structures.

To plan for future development, the master plan proposes a flexible system to allow for incremental change and replacement, all of which must also comply with the goals of the university master plan and the Town of Chapel Hill's progressive zoning laws and limited-growth policies.

3 Medical Education Quadrangle
4 Master plan buildout
5 Medical research aerial

3

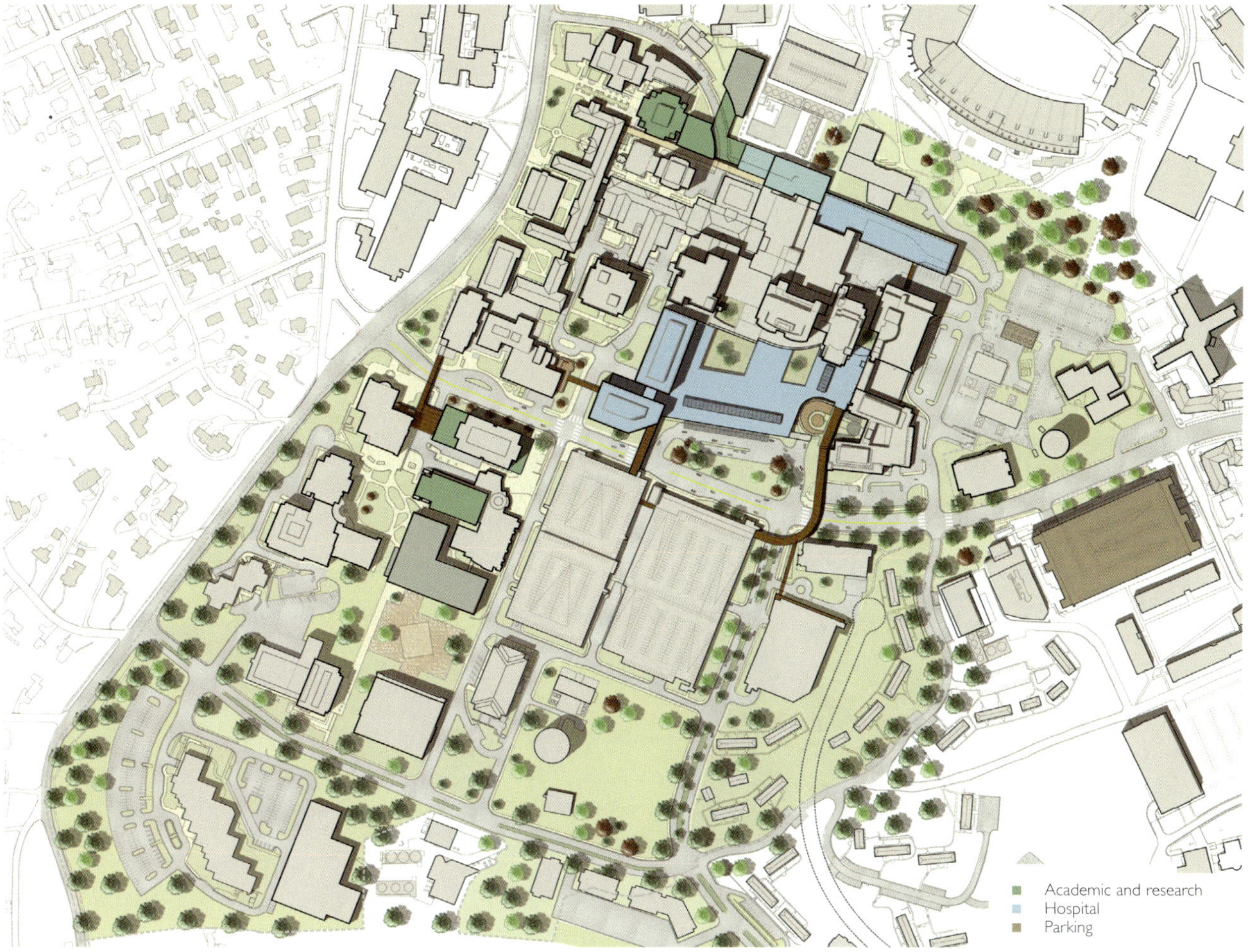

4

5

1

Location	Philadelphia, Pennsylvania
Completion	2006
Size	3,000,000 square feet

The Children's Hospital of Philadelphia

South Campus Master Plan

1 South Campus aerial from southwest
2 Ambulatory Care Center perspective

2

Consistently ranked among the top children's hospitals in the United States, The Children's Hospital of Philadelphia (CHOP) is committed to securing its reputation with a world-class campus that supports and expands its clinical and research activities.

The site for the South Campus master plan, a 7.9-acre parcel directly adjacent to CHOP's existing North Campus, provides an opportunity to create a fully translational medical platform that fosters direct connections between daily patient care and research. This bench-to-bedside model is designed to help speed the discovery of new diagnostic and therapeutic tools. The master plan provides for service neighborhoods, or care clusters, that offer convenience for patients and their families while enhancing collegiality among physicians and scientists.

The project comprises three key elements: a 3 million-square-foot master plan; programming and schematic design of a 1 million-square-foot infrastructure plinth containing parking, a central receiving dock, and research support space; and programming and schematic design of a 500,000-square-foot ambulatory care building and a 300,000-square-foot research building.

Employing an organization-wide approach that also considers the existing North Campus, the master plan assesses CHOP's overall needs, taking into consideration the probable need for future reorganization and growth as well as the financial demands of running a premier healthcare facility. Short-term management scenarios suggested optimizing existing buildings, while longer-term scenarios studied the demolition of existing buildings over time, creating the opportunity to introduce new, leading-edge construction.

This project will be flanked by major ambulatory care and research developments for the University of Pennsylvania Health System, a proximity that will support collaboration and the sharing of cancer treatment facilities between the two health institutions.

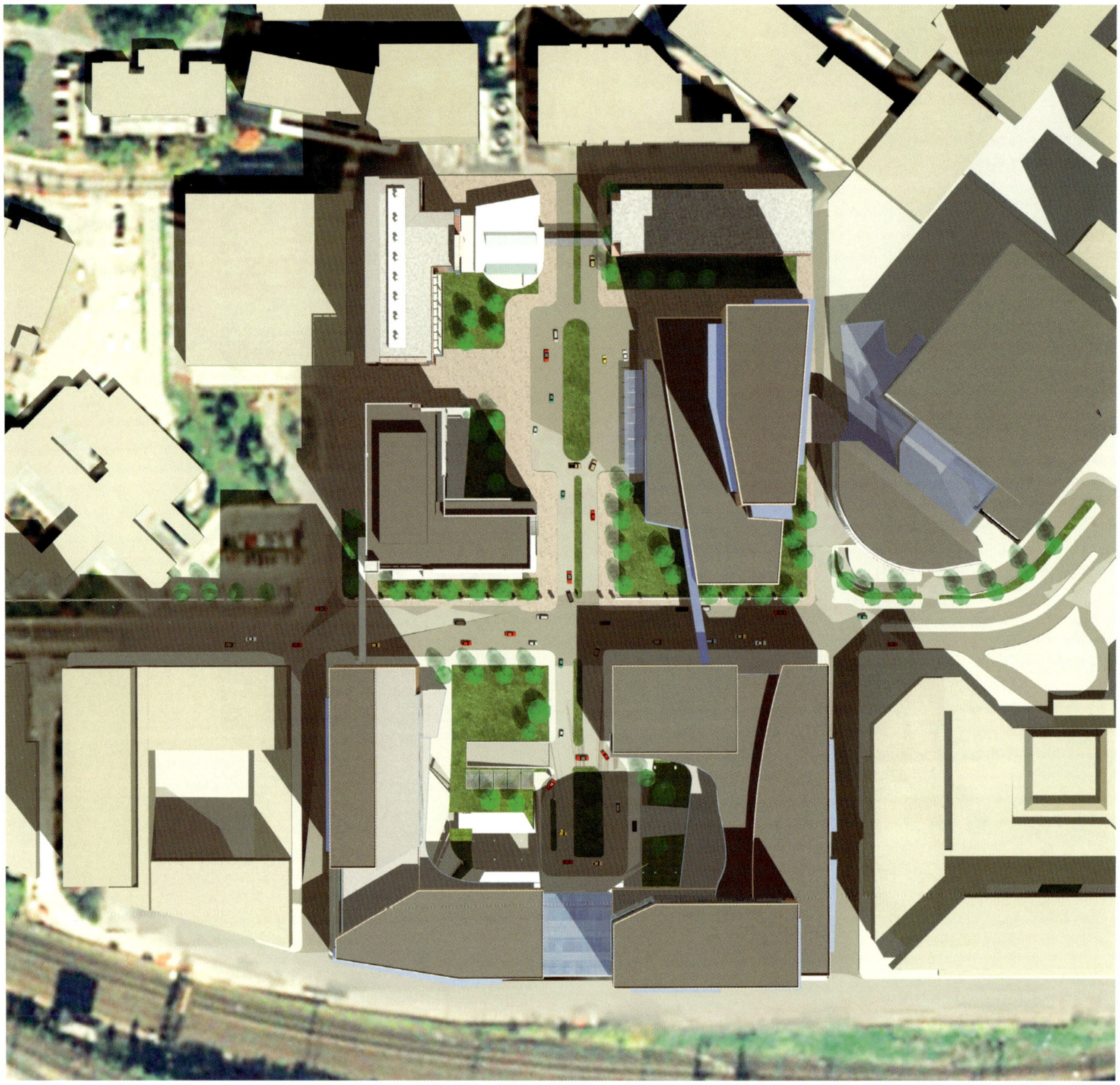

3

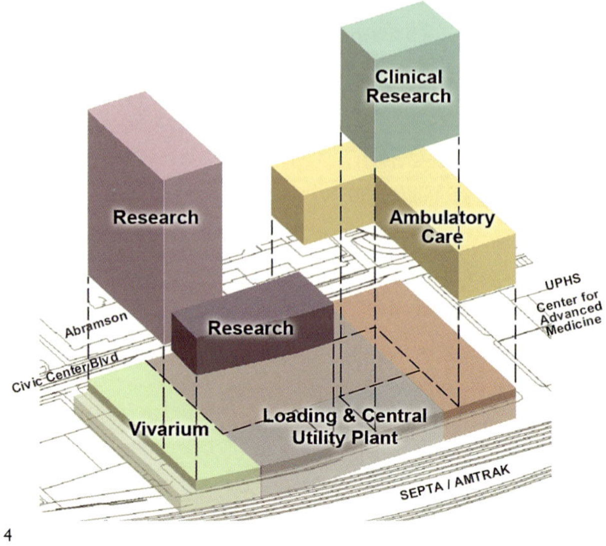

4

3 North and South Campus aerial
4 Axonometric
5&6 Concept sketches

5

6

PITAL OF PHILADELPHIA

8

9

Opposite:
View of North Campus from South Campus green
8 Ambulatory Care Center model
9 South Campus aerial from southeast

1 Arrival
2 Master plan buildout

1

Location	Cleveland, Ohio
Completion	2006
Size	14,401,000 square feet

The Cleveland Clinic Foundation

Master Plan

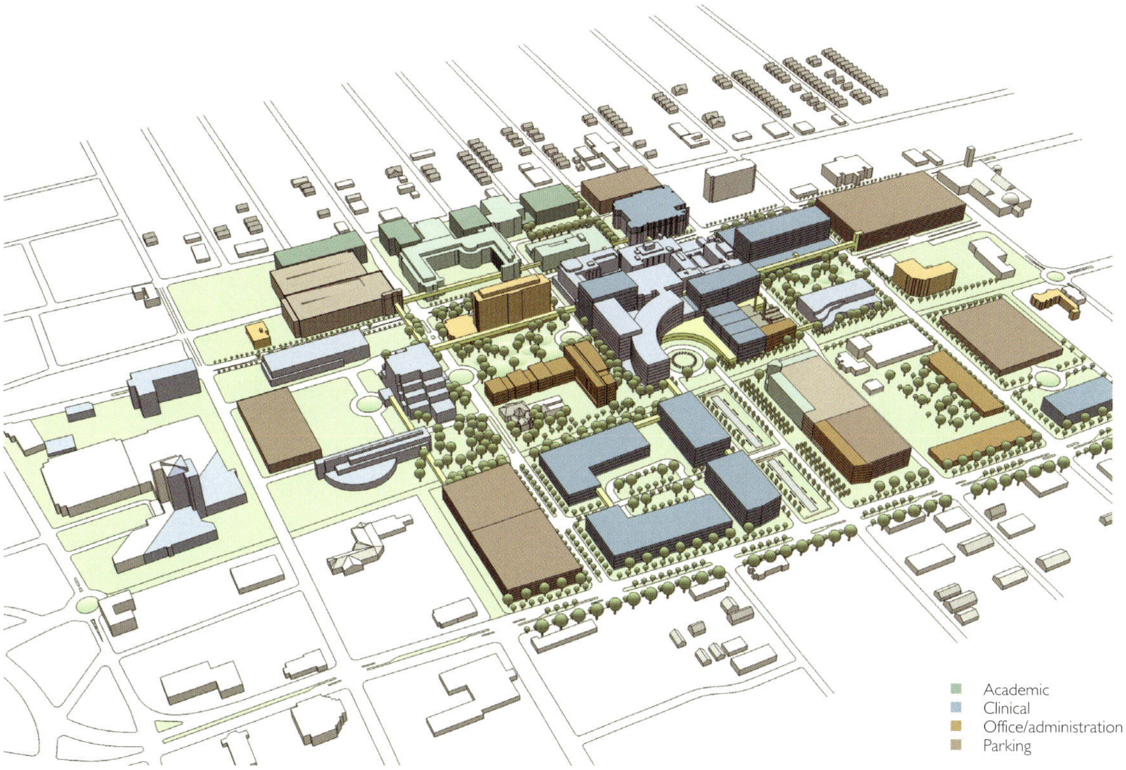

2

The Cleveland Clinic main campus occupies a gateway site along Cleveland's historic Euclid Avenue and anchors the western edge of the University Circle district, the educational and cultural heart of the city. Along with The Cleveland Clinic, this district includes marquee institutions such as Case Western Reserve University, University Hospitals of Cleveland, The Cleveland Museum of Art, The Cleveland Orchestra, and Rockefeller Park, which links north to Lake Erie. The master plan proposes to organize the campus for significant long-term growth and building replacement while strengthening its pivotal position in the broader urban fabric.

Projections for significant hospital growth combined with the need to replace core facilities over time call for the reconfiguration of patient and visitor access and vehicular, pedestrian, and service traffic. The new circulation plan relocates the hospital entrance to improve visibility and convenience for staff, patients, and visitors while allowing the campus to better accommodate the city's nascent plan to enhance Euclid Avenue as a public transportation spine with limited private automobile use.

The campus is organized around distinct ambulatory and inpatient zones, each with clear arrival and parking patterns. Landscaped footpaths replace surface parking areas, creating a pedestrian-friendly experience. An employee parking and service zone is established at the campus perimeter to reduce congestion and link to the core of the campus through a dedicated below-grade concourse that will minimize disruption as adjacent sites are developed.

1 Health Sciences Medical Education Center
2 College of Nursing
3 Health Sciences Administration
4 College of Medicine
5 School of Public Health
6 Dentistry expansion
7 College of Dentistry
8 College of Optometry

1

2

Location	Columbus, Ohio
Completion	2005
Size	7,000,000 square feet

1 Health sciences district
2 Health sciences academic campus
3 Concept sketch

The Ohio State University Medical Center

Master Site and Facilities Plan

3

The Ohio State University Medical Center is one of just a few academic medical center campuses on which the medical center is co-located with all of the health sciences colleges as well as the university itself. This master plan represents a long-term vision to conceive and develop a true 21st-century "health sciences environment" in which teaching, learning, research, and clinical care flourish through interdisciplinary collaboration among clinics and colleges.

Over the next 10 to 20 years, Ohio State's health sciences community expects growth that calls for a doubling of built space on the medical center campus. To accommodate this growth in a climate of evolving teaching, clinical service, and research models, the master plan proposes a strategically phased approach that employs incremental replacement and reorganization of many of the buildings on its 75-acre campus, including those for the Colleges of Medicine, Dentistry, Optometry, Nursing, and the School of Public Health. Every successfully implemented phase will result in an operational medical center that will be augmented by each subsequent phase.

The master plan sites research facilities together to provide numerous efficiencies and collegiality, also creating a dual adjacency to each discipline's clinical counterpart (for example, cancer research center and cancer hospital) to promote Ohio State's commitment to the translational medical model that thrives on the physical proximity between research and clinical treatment. Older buildings between the research and clinical facilities no longer programmed for their original use house dry research, faculty offices, and administrative centers—areas that require little to refurbish and maintain—allowing the wet research and clinical areas to absorb the majority of Ohio State's capital investment.

The new Health Sciences district adjoins the Medical Center to the south and sites each college with a strong, individual presence on the new Health Sciences quadrangle. The centerpiece of this quadrangle is a Medical Education Center that houses shared teaching laboratories, classrooms, amenities, and technology needed to support increasingly interdisciplinary teaching programs.

A health education zone is created in the southwest section of the Health Sciences district, proximal to existing education facilities. Future spaces for the College of Medicine are categorized as dedicated, flexible, or shared. Dedicated space includes classrooms, laboratories, and offices; flexible space is designed to expand capacity for programs as needed; and shared space is intended for use by all of the health sciences colleges and provides opportunities for increased interaction between students and faculty.

Due to its large scope, the entire vision for this campus can only be realized over multiple phases. Strategic priorities dictate an initial focus on hospital expansion in which the clinical base is extended and fully integrated between existing and new spaces. This early-phase development forms a research and clinical core that can be extended by redevelopment of the Health Sciences district and development of a 30-acre parcel for clinical and research expansion.

4 Master plan buildout
5 Medical center from southwest
6 Medical center expansion and access
7 Medical center and health sciences academic campuses

4

5

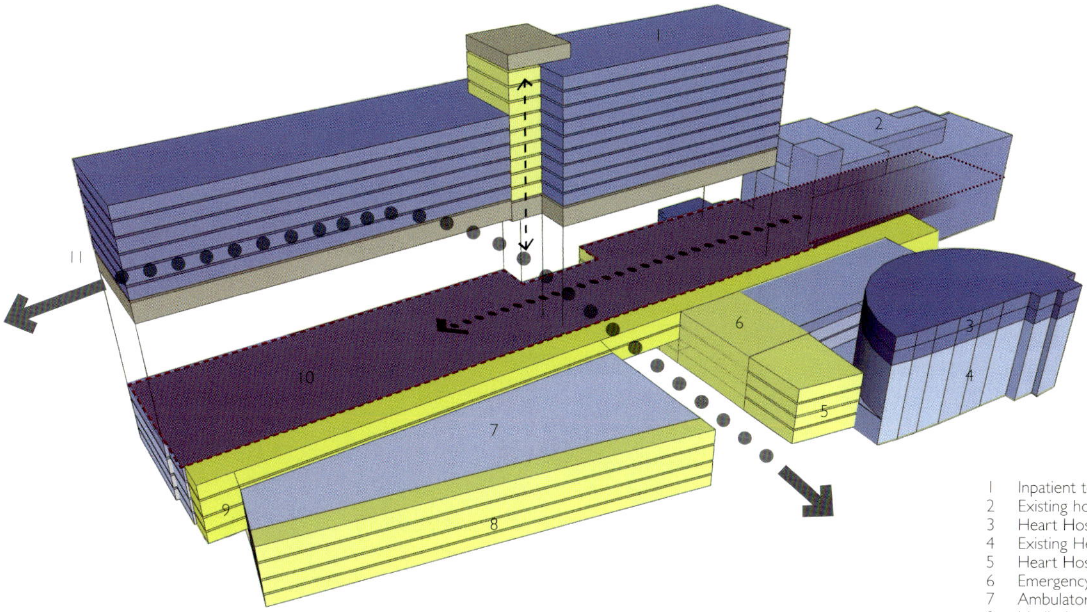

6

1 Inpatient towers
2 Existing hospital
3 Heart Hospital expansion
4 Existing Heart Hospital
5 Heart Hospital atrium
6 Emergency Care Pavilion
7 Ambulatory services
8 Medical center entry concourse
9 Main connector concourse
10 Diagnostic and treatment platform
11 Campus circulation link

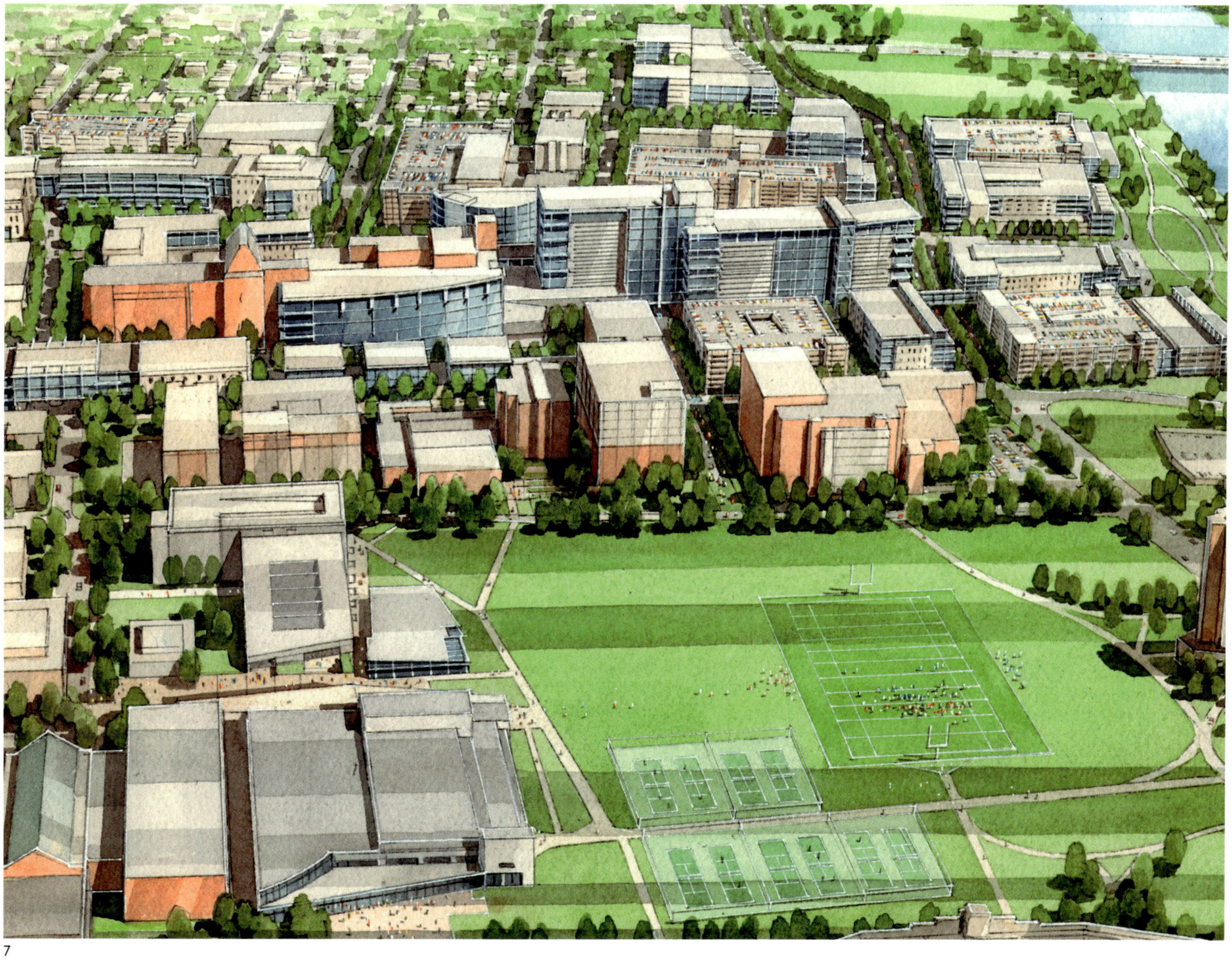

7

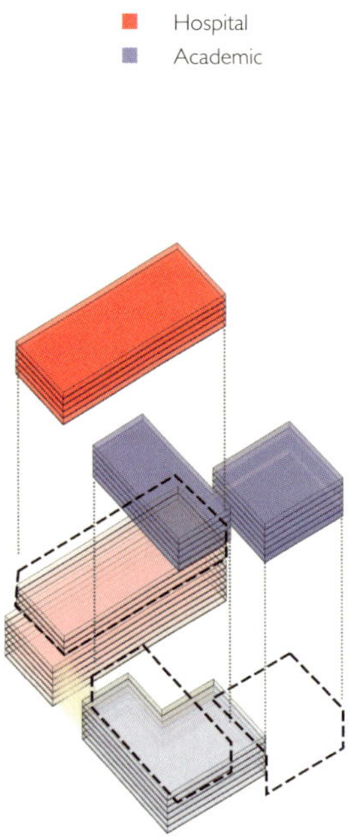

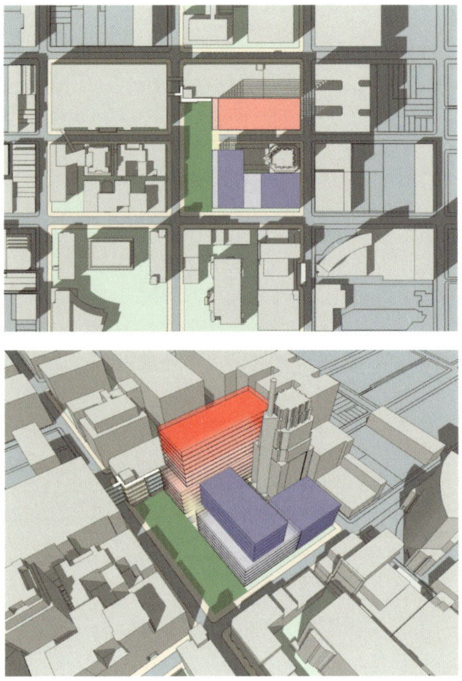

1

2

Location	Philadelphia, Pennsylvania
Completion	2006
Size	3,500,000 square feet

Thomas Jefferson University and Thomas Jefferson University Hospital

Master Plan

1 Urban context
2 Jefferson Square
3 Concept sketch of Jefferson Square

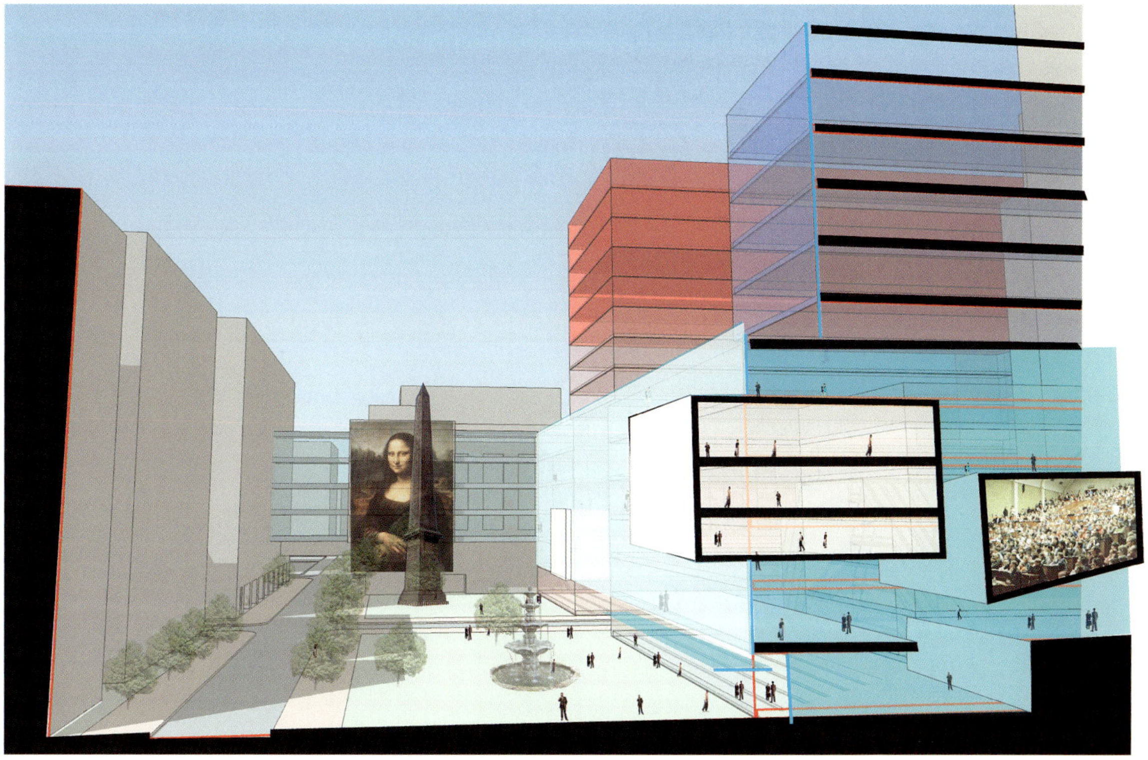

3

This master plan creates a campus vision that integrates clinical and academic functions and provides a roadmap for future facility growth, restoration, and modernization at Thomas Jefferson University and Thomas Jefferson University Hospital (Jefferson). Together, the two institutions comprise approximately 3.5 million square feet of built space distributed over nine city blocks in the heart of Center City Philadelphia.

The Center City district was laid out by William Penn in 1682, with streets aligned on a grid, an open square in the middle, and a park-like square in each of four quadrants. Jefferson occupies a unique position within the district's historic grid. The site is bracketed to the east by the old city—Society Hill, Washington and Independence Squares, lower Market Street, and the surrounding residential areas—and to the west by a more modern, high-rise financial district. To the south, the site is bordered by the low-rise, residential Washington Square neighborhood, and to the north by the commercial and retail convention center district.

The Jefferson campus lies at the epicenter of these distinctive urban neighborhoods and includes buildings with architectural styles that span the entire 20th century. While it incorporates aspects of many of its varied contexts, it neither commits itself to any single border identity nor develops its own inviting sense of place. Through restrained massing, landscaping, sensitivity to context, and the implementation of easy-to-navigate circulation paths, Jefferson's clinical and academic ambitions can be realized while also offering an enduring moment in the overall urban fabric.

To that end, the master plan proposes the development of a new generation of academic buildings fronted by a new Center City urban plaza, colloquially referred to as "Jefferson Square." Along with the new Hamilton Academic Plaza, this square will provide a cohesive center of gravity for the university and hospital while also serving as a public amenity that unifies the campus within its broader Center City context. Underscoring the East Development and Jefferson Square, Walnut Street between 9th and 11th Streets will be developed into an east–west green axis. Jefferson Square will be a key destination on Walnut Street, bringing open space to both the Jefferson community and the growing residential and retail communities in the immediate area. Preliminary design concepts incorporate active public functions such as retail stores and spaces for interpretive art, as well as restful green spaces reminiscent of Penn's 1682 plan.

On the Boards

1

2

3

Location	Waltham, Massachusetts
Completion	2008
Size	200,000 square feet

1 Concept sketch
2 Exterior view
3 View from Route 128
4 Lobby

Boston Properties
77 CityPoint

4

This Class-A suburban office building is located on Route 128, a semi-circular freeway that rings Metro Boston and is often referred to as "America's Technology Highway." The facility houses various high-technology tenants and offers numerous amenities, including a leading-edge conference center, buffet restaurant, exterior plaza, and in-house fitness center. The project also includes a seven-story parking garage.

Sited at the top of a hill, the curved structure responds to the sloping topography and provides tenants and visitors with dramatic views of neighboring towns and the well-traveled highway. Its six-story façade, composed of articulated white precast concrete and lightly reflective clear glass, creates a sweeping presence on the hill. Two vertical towers clad in a darker glass curtainwall are situated at the building corners to balance its horizontality. A large glass canopy announces the entrance into a two-story lobby.

Consideration toward sustainability and environmental impact guided the building design. The building is the first project in suburban Boston to achieve LEED Core and Shell silver pre-certification from the U.S. Green Building Council.

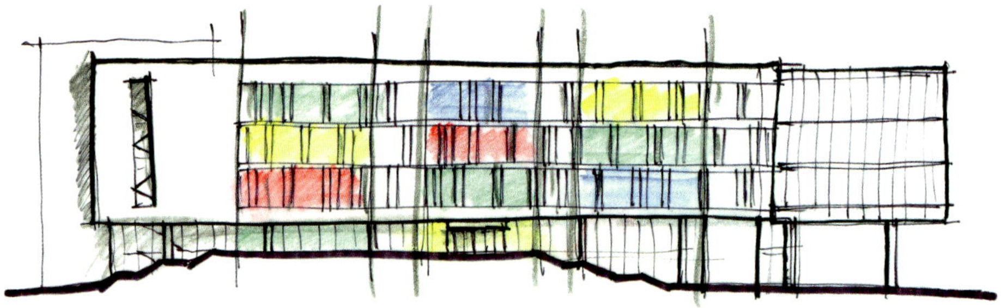

1

2

Location	Providence, Rhode Island
Completion	2009
Size	82,000 square feet

1 Concept sketch
2 Campus approach
3 Lobby

Johnson & Wales University

Culinary Arts Building

3

As the first new building in Johnson & Wales University's master plan for its Harborside campus, this project will set the tone and direction for future development. The building is expected to receive LEED certification from the U. S. Green Building Council.

Adjacent to a culinary arts museum and expected to be a popular tour destination for the university, the building offers maximum transparency to showcase and celebrate the school's culinary program. Key instructional spaces of the building include a diverse range of kitchen labs, a leading-edge wine tasting room, and various types of instructional dining facilities.

The exterior of the building is scaled and massed carefully so that it complements existing structures while presenting a clear identity that announces itself as a public space. Various material types and textures create a welcoming skin for this facility that is both learning institution and observation center. Labs, classrooms, and corridors are configured to offer students and faculty enough privacy to achieve an optimal learning experience even as visitors look on. The dean's suite is designed as a glass box lined with wine bottles and features an integrated conference/presentation room that hovers dramatically over the main lobby to illuminate the artistic aspect of the culinary experience. New academic offices on multiple floors integrate the faculty with student traffic and activity.

The building is sited on 100 acres of a former shipyard in a designated flood zone. Anticipating regular rising water, all programmed areas in the structure are lifted above the 12-foot flood clearance line. A shallow earth terrace resolves into a graceful staircase that accentuates the building's elevated entrance. For added safety in the event of a flood, the lower walls incorporate breakaway technology to allow for the free flow of water.

In addition to addressing flood concerns, the raising of the building creates a covered open space at the street level that is conducive to many year-round outdoor public events, including ice carving. The open space also unifies the other campus greens that now reach out to a main intersection, creating lawns and pedestrian footpaths where building corners are expected. The height of the building and the lifting of its entry floors also provide students, faculty, staff, and visitors with unrestricted and sweeping views of nearby Narragansett Bay.

4 Elevation
5 North-south elevations
6 Level two floor plan
7 Level three floor plan
8 Level four floor plan

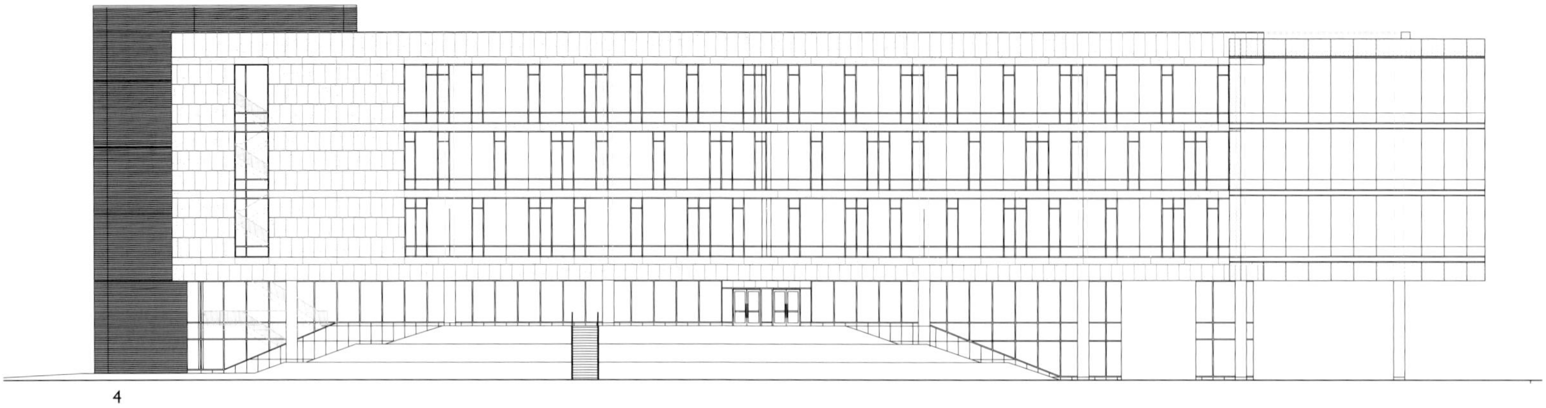

4

5

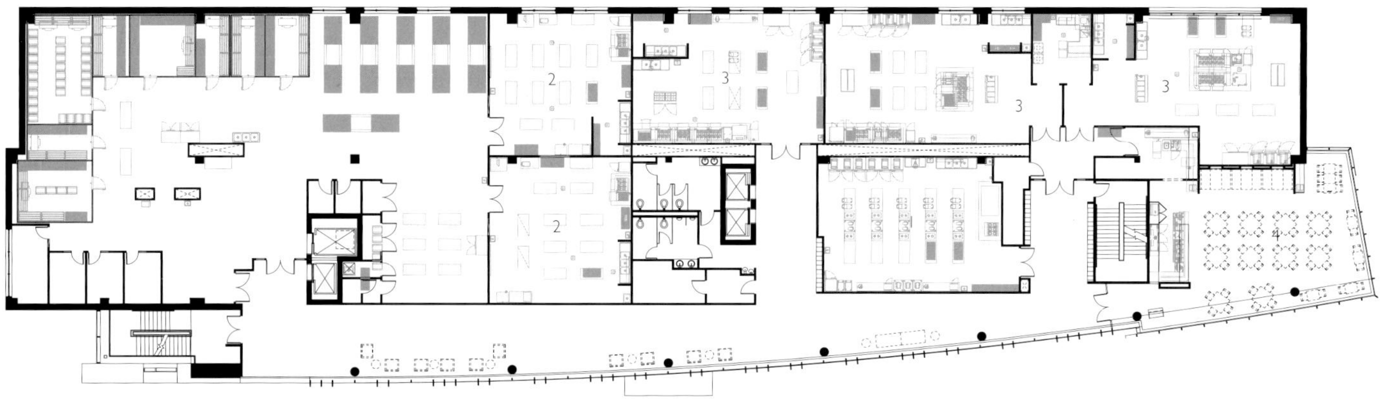

6

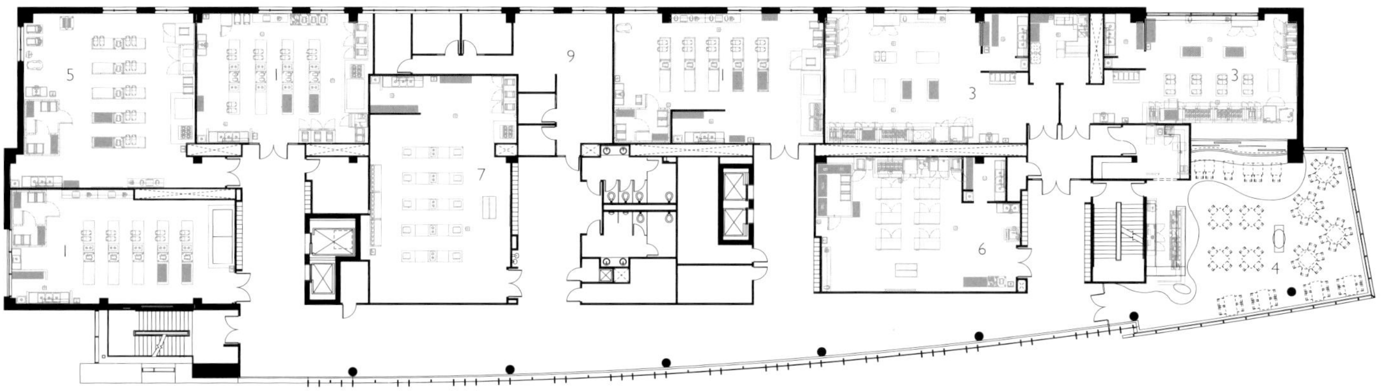

7

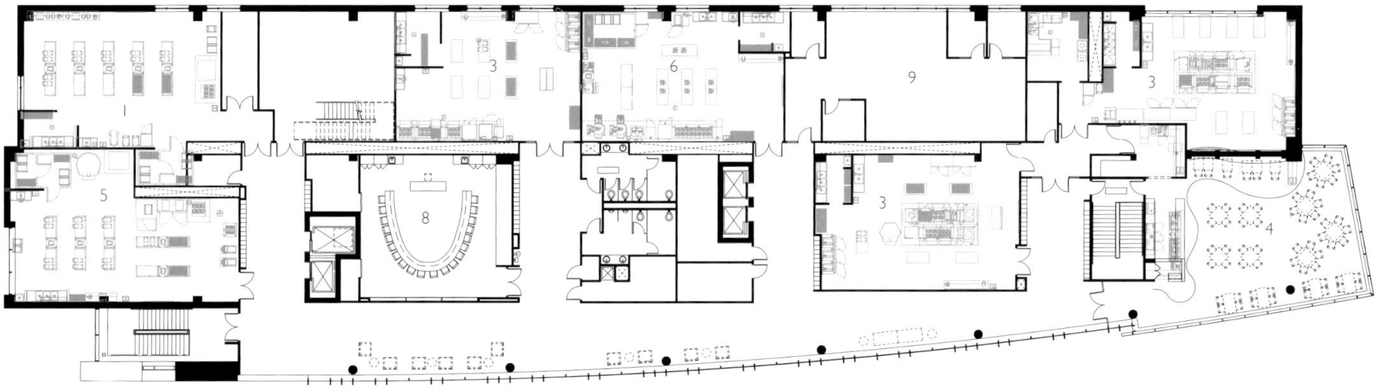

8

1 Pastry lab
2 Meat room
3 Hot kitchen
4 Dining room
5 Bake lab
6 Garde manger
7 Chocolate lab
8 Wine lab
9 Office

9

10

11

9 Dining room
10&11 Interior concept boards

1 Aerial perspective
2 Great Hall entry

1

Location	St. Louis, Missouri
Completion	2008
Size	114,000 square feet

Washington University in St. Louis

The William H. and Elizabeth Gray Danforth University Center

2

Washington University in St. Louis' growing prominence as one of the nation's top 12 research universities calls for a new university center that welcomes and celebrates every participant in its academic life: students, faculty, staff, alumni, neighbors, parents, friends, and visiting dignitaries.

This 21st-century-ready facility provides a new front door and a new public face for the university. The center serves as a campus crossroads, offering three outdoor courtyards and plazas as well as interior meeting rooms, office space, lounges, and a range of dining venues. In keeping with Washington University's signature Collegiate Gothic style, the exterior responds to the principles of interlocking spaces and forms laid forth in the Cope & Stewardson campus plan.

The three-story building, which sits atop an underground parking garage, is centrally located on the campus and is accessible by St. Louis' Metrolink public transportation system, fortifying the Danforth University Center's identity as a hub for campus activity. The south side of the building features a public drop-off space for visitors and a formal entry hall, and the north side offers a less formal entrance for students and other members of the university community.

The contemporary interior is warm, inviting, and generously sized. The dining hall and the Commons Area, which includes a massive fireplace, dominate the first floor and offer a range of social spaces for convening and interacting. Also included on the first floor is a career center that features conference and seminar rooms along with office space. The second level includes classrooms, a "fun room" for students, and a formal lounge that overlooks the Commons. The third floor contains the graduate center and serves as the communications hub for the student community, housing the student-run TV and radio stations as well as the offices of the student newspaper, yearbook, and other print media.

The building was designed with consideration toward sustainability and environmental impact. It is expected to receive LEED gold certification from the U. S. Green Building Council.

3

4

3 Concept sketch
4 Student entry
5 Main level plan

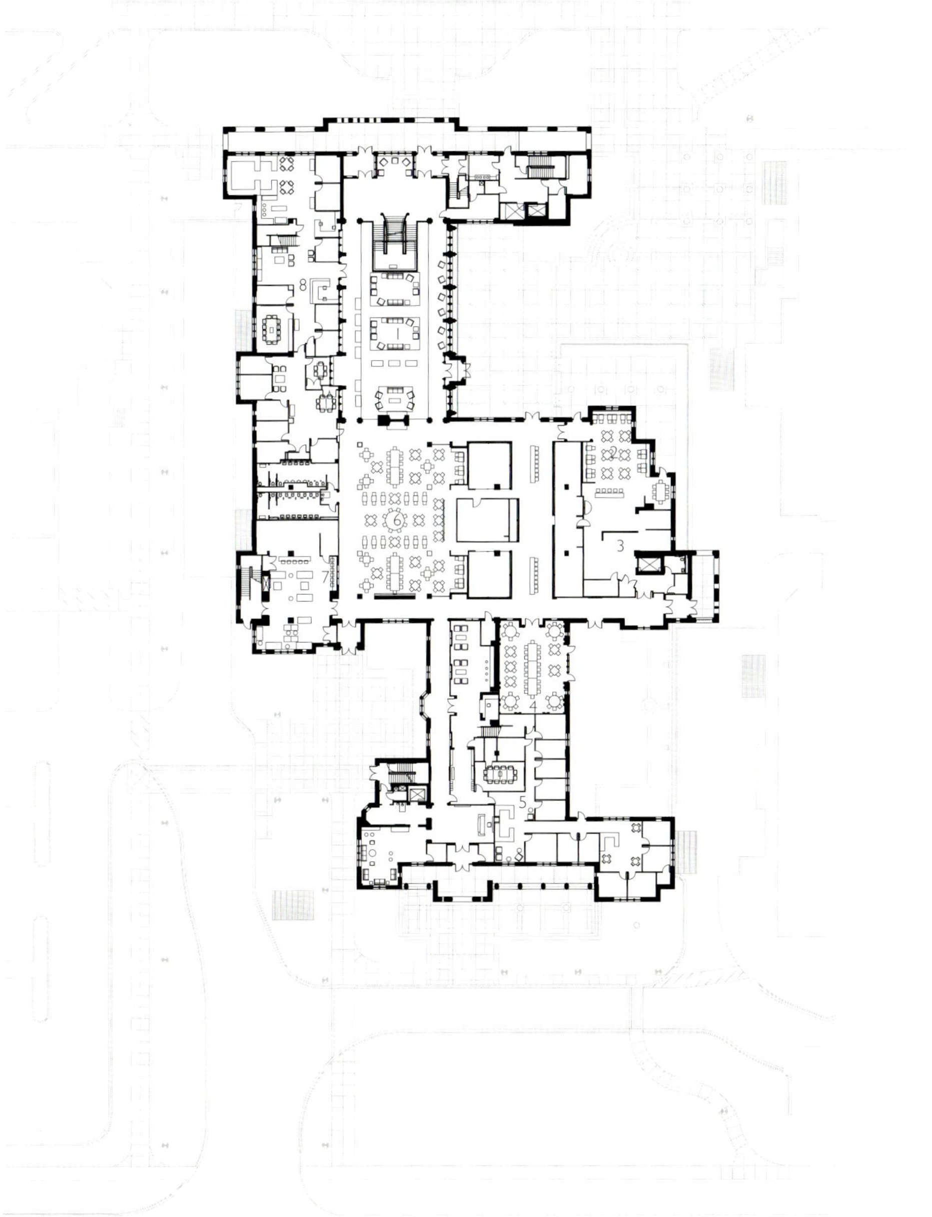

5

1 Commons
2 Bistro
3 Kitchen
4 Formal dining
5 Career center
6 Student dining
7 Café
8 Campus life

6

7

6 Concept sketch
7 Student plaza
8 Great Hall

8

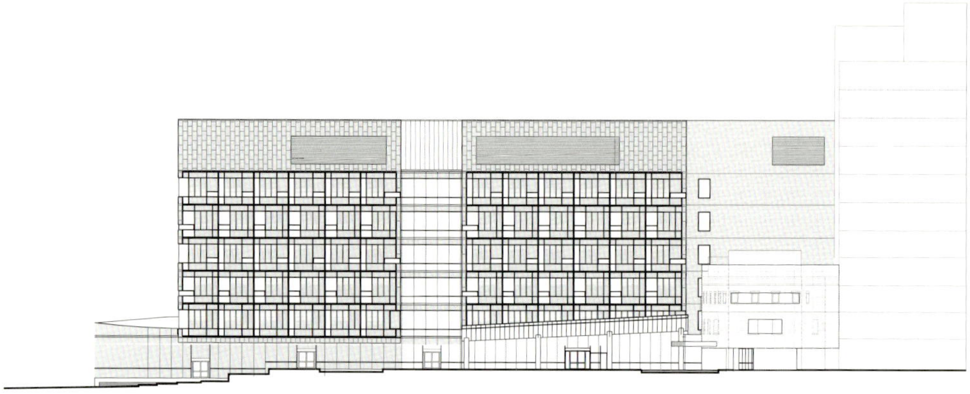

1

2

1 East elevation
2 View from Riverside Avenue
3 Family Resource Center
Following pages:
West façade

Location	Minneapolis, Minnesota
Completion	2010
Size	353,100 square feet
	25,350 square feet (renovation)

University of Minnesota Children's Hospital, Fairview

Replacement Hospital

3

As the first step in a comprehensive and complex phasing strategy to upgrade its facilities, the University of Minnesota Children's Hospital, Fairview is building a replacement hospital on its Riverside campus. The nine-story building will bring a leading-edge pediatric care center to Minneapolis while supporting Fairview's research and patient- and family-centered care objectives. In addition, the project includes underground parking, a new Pediatric Emergency Department, and an expansion of Fairview's existing imaging department and surgical suite.

The plan calls for a distinctive identity for Fairview while also ensuring a coherent, unified campus where the wayfinding makes navigation easy for patients, staff, and visitors. The massing and organization of the building reinforces the street edge and provides a prominent presence for Fairview along the main thoroughfare of Riverside Avenue. A one-story glass façade welcomes incoming visitors.

The building is organized by four neighborhoods of nursing units that are autonomous towers clustered at each corner. Interstitial areas that house the family lounge, playroom, and staff education room connect the towers. Natural light penetrates through these areas into the floor plate, illuminating the daily activities of patients, visitors, and staff. The transparency of the interstitial space on the south façade also promotes an urban connection between the hospital and the community, while the spaces on the east and west provide views and natural light.

Inpatient rooms, examination rooms, and procedure spaces are designed to accommodate and encourage family participation in a child's healing process. Diagnostic and testing services are located near their corresponding clinics and bed floors to improve patient experience and increase staff efficiency.

5 Daylight study
6 Grand stair
7 Team station
8 Patient room

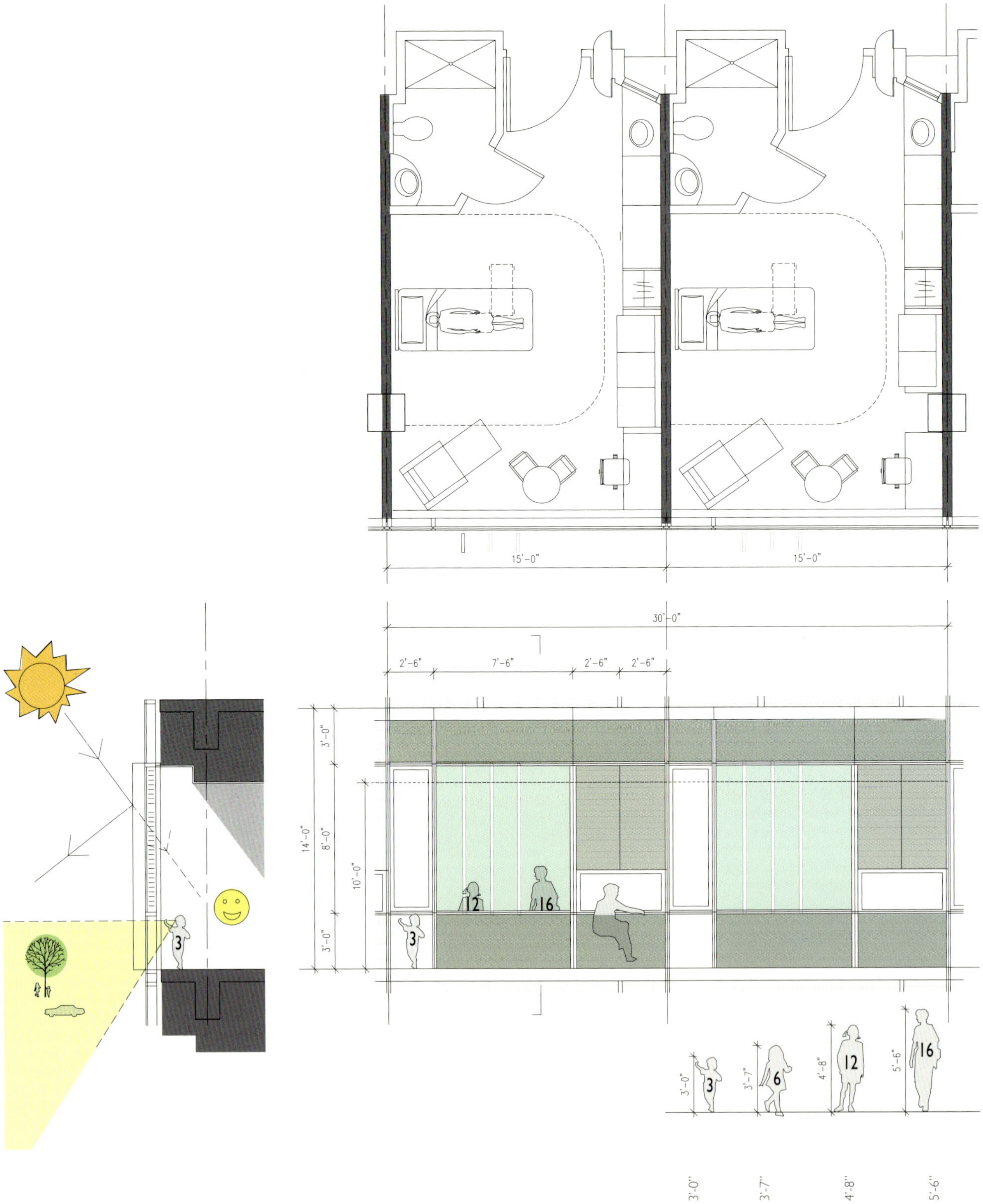

5

6

7

8

1

Location	Boston, Massachusetts
Completion	2011
Size	245,000 square feet

1 View from Albany Street
2 Main lobby

Boston Medical Center

Carl J. and Ruth Shapiro Ambulatory Care Center

2

The latest in a series of strategic development and planning initiatives by Boston Medical Center, the Shapiro Center embodies the hospital's mission to provide "exceptional care without exception." Located on a highly visible site, the nine-story building represents the first phase in a long-term effort by Boston Medical Center to transform the image of its Albany Street campus edge. The building will set the stage for future improvements along Albany Street, including a provision for better pedestrian access and a better-defined, active street edge.

The scale and proportions of the building are sympathetic to the surrounding context, providing relief from the built density of the campus. A terracotta cladding system on the exterior skin introduces a contemporary counterpoint to the traditional brick façades found across the existing campus. In keeping with Boston Medical Center's precedent of balancing buildings with open space, the covered entry drive creates an urban city court, with patterned brick pavers and landscaping that can be viewed from within the lobby waiting areas.

The building's interior utilizes a palette of warm materials and colors that evokes the natural environment. The terracotta cladding of the exterior is brought inside and provides a bold accent in the composition of the two-story lobby. A contemplative garden of bamboo and river rock also blurs the separation of interior and exterior space and provides a backdrop to an inviting monumental stair that leads to a second-level café. Cream-colored terrazzo flooring, sandblasted glass, and a wood ceiling also contribute to a welcoming and calming environment.

The modular planning of the clinical floors optimizes flexibility and improves wayfinding, and a perimeter corridor with a southern exposure provides access to the various clinics and offers orienting views to the world outside. Clinic waiting rooms organized off the corridor also benefit from natural views and light, which is filtered through patterned glass that recalls the bamboo garden in the lobby. Inside the clinics, clear organization and a simple circulation system ease patient and staff use, with corridors arranged to provide direct or indirect access to daylight.

Poised to set a new standard for sustainable design among Boston healthcare facilities, the Shapiro Center employs environmentally sensitive materials and technologies including a variety of energy-efficient and water-conserving features for mechanical, electrical, and architectural systems. The building is registered as a pilot project with the *Green Guide for Healthcare,* with a targeted U. S. Green Building Council LEED silver rating equivalent.

Opposite:
View from East Concord Street
4 Entry
5 Corridor

4

5

6 Site plan
7 Study models

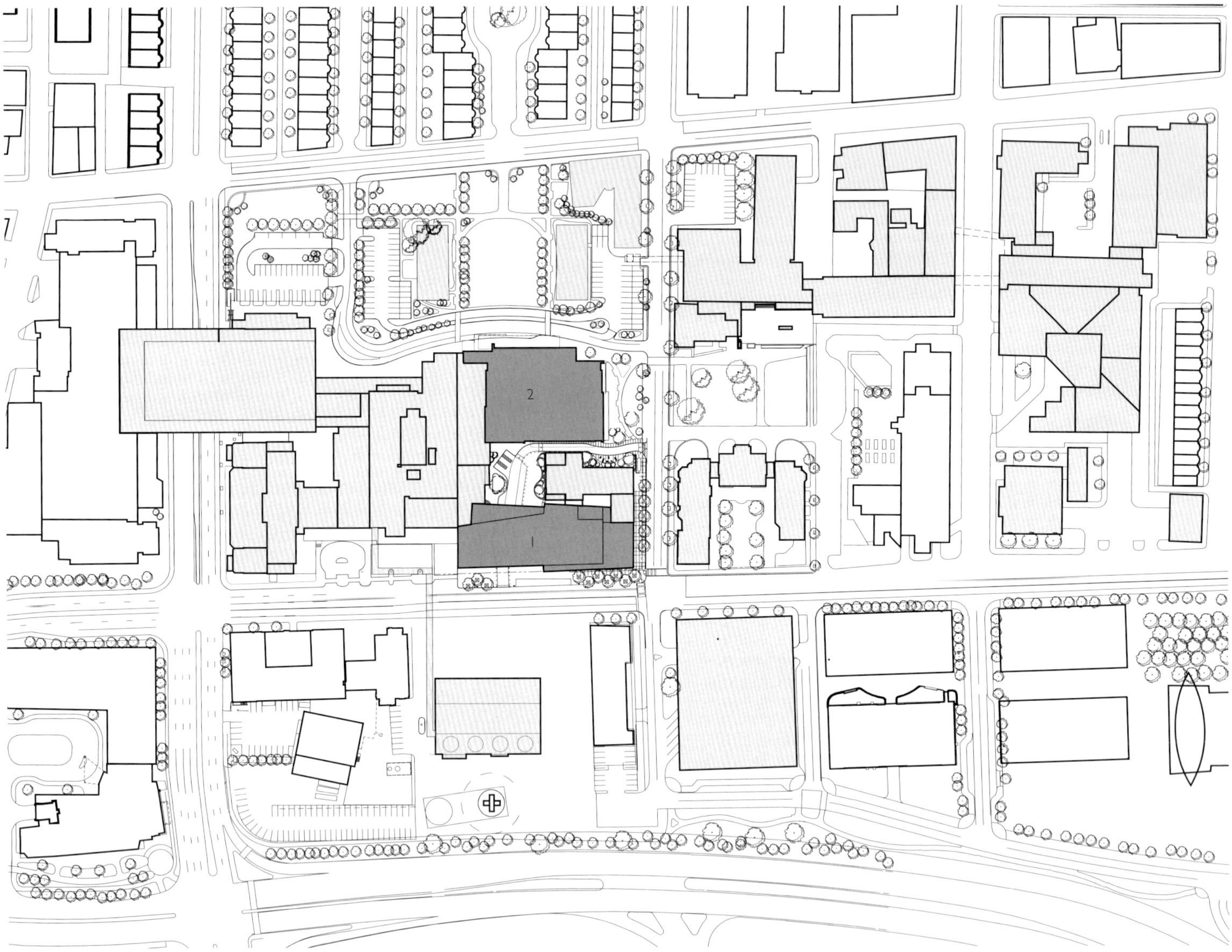

6

1 Carl J. and Ruth Shapiro Ambulatory Care Center
2 Moakley Building

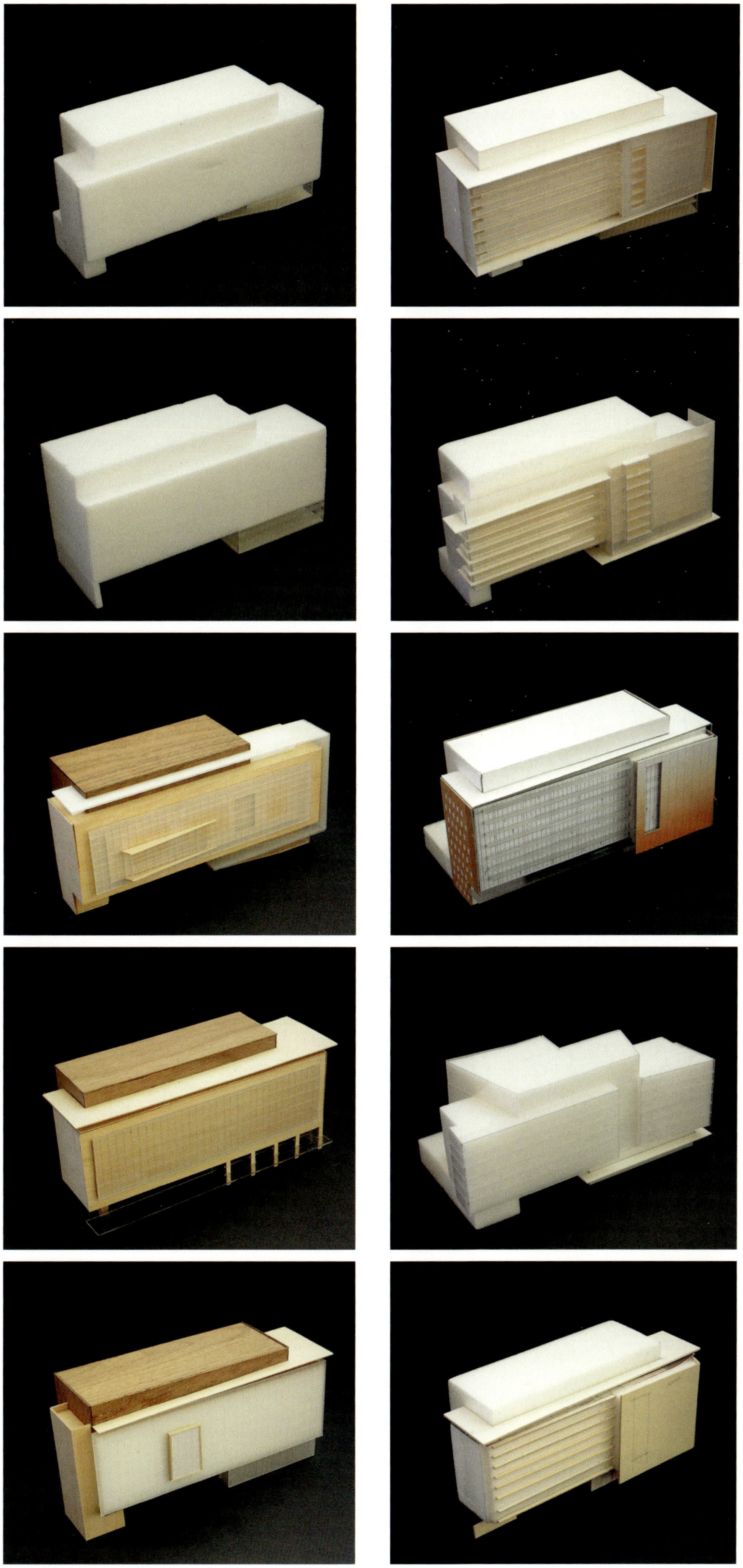

7

1

Location	Oklahoma City, Oklahoma
Completion	2008
Size	53,630 square feet

1 Entry detail
2 Lobby

ProCure Treatment Centers
Oklahoma ProCure Treatment Center

2

This proton therapy center is the first installation of a prototype that ProCure intends to adapt for multiple locations across the United States. Located on a four-acre site just outside of Oklahoma City at the gateway to a new medical office complex, the facility incorporates full views of the downtown area.

The center contains four treatment rooms—one rotating gantry, one fixed horizontal beam, and two inclined beams. Together they will be capable of treating 12 patients per hour. To support this high volume, the building features an efficient organizational layout that achieves peak operational capacity. In addition, the facility is designed to accommodate future expansion as needed. Many human-scaled details are employed to demonstrate sensitivity to the patient experience in this highly technical environment.

The building's dynamic façade features a series of simple stone planes punctuated by sections of glazing that offer views to the interior public areas while connecting the interior to the surrounding landscape. A subtle curve at the front of the building provides contemporary scale and presents a welcoming image for patients and visitors. A narrowly profiled canopy lifts away from the building mass to announce the entry.

Inside, the building is designed to evoke a spa-like ambience of comfort and healing. A two-story, sun-filled reception and waiting area greets patients, families, and staff and overlooks an outdoor garden. A continuous skylight bathes the patient treatment corridor in light, which also spills into the secondary waiting areas and treatment room entrances. A simple palette of natural materials including fieldstone, limestone, and cherry combined with subtle colors and indirect lighting work together to create a feeling of warmth and elegance that belies the technology-intensive nature of the facility.

3

3 Entry approach
4&5 Interior concept boards
6 Treatment room

4

5

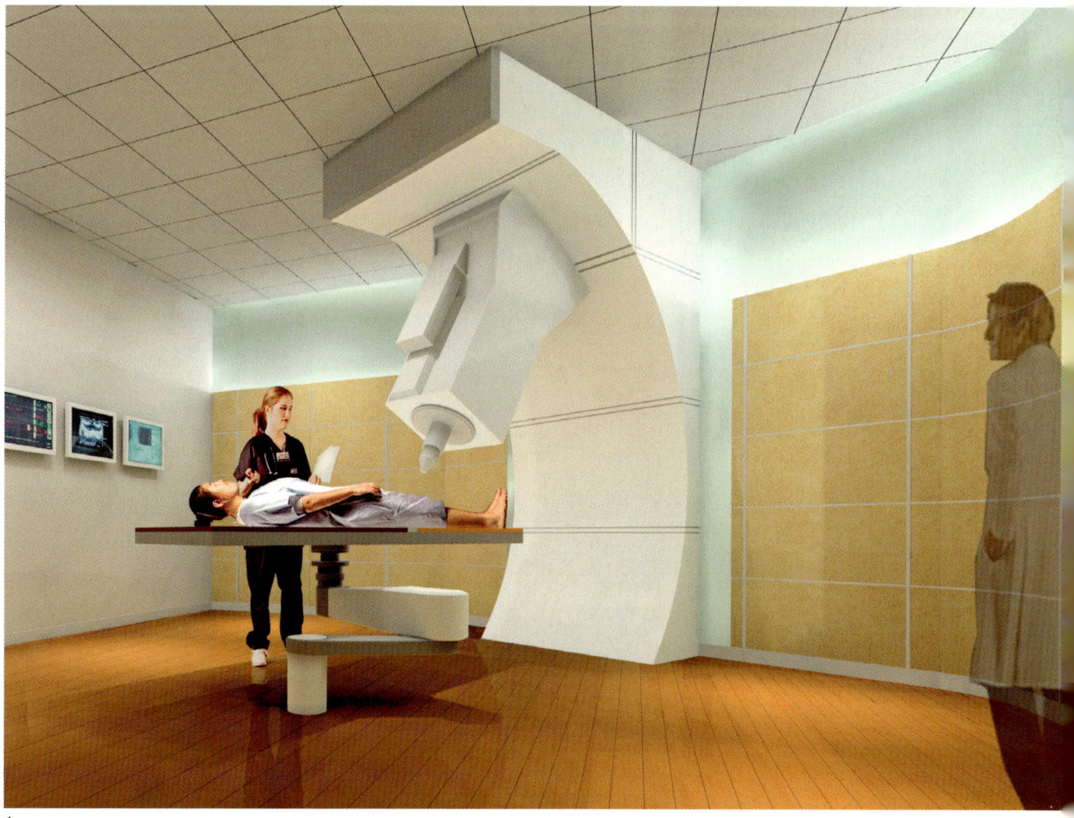

6

Timeline and Credits

Timeline

1983

Brigham and Women's Hospital
Ambulatory Services Building II, Boston, MA

Brigham and Women's Hospital
Eugene Braunwald Research Center, Boston, MA

Brigham and Women's Hospital
Master Plan, Boston, MA

Harvard Medical School
Master Plan, Lab Standards, and Quadrangle Renovations, Boston, MA

Lotus Development Corporation
Corporate Headquarters, Cambridge, MA

Lotus Development Corporation
One Canal Park, Cambridge, MA

New England Medical Center
Master Plan, Boston, MA

The Acushnet Company
Titleist Plant, Dartmouth, MA

Brigham and Women's Hospital

Harvard Medical School

Lotus Development Corporation

1990

Ames Safety Envelope Company
Corporate Headquarters, Somerville, MA

Beth Israel Deaconess Medical Center
Research North, Boston, MA

Brigham and Women's Hospital
Center for Women and Newborns, Boston, MA

Brigham and Women's Hospital
Coronary Care ICU, Boston, MA

Brigham and Women's Hospital
Emergency Department, Boston, MA

Brigham and Women's Hospital
Interventional Magnetic Resonance Facility, Boston, MA

Brigham and Women's Hospital
Medical Oncology Suite, Boston, MA

Brigham and Women's Hospital
Tower Lobby and Entry Drive Renovations, Boston, MA

Bytex Corporation
Corporate Headquarters, Westborough, MA

Faulkner Hospital
Physicians' Office Building, Boston, MA

HCI (Scotland) Ltd.
Hospital Interiors, Clydebank, Scotland

HCI (Scotland) Ltd.
The Beardmore Hotel, Clydebank, Scotland

Lucent Technologies
Corporate Offices, Concord, MA

Marine Biological Resources Center
Marine Biological Laboratory, Woods Hole, MA

Massachusetts Water Resources Authority
Water Treatment Plant, Boston, MA

MIT Real Estate
640 Memorial Drive, Cambridge, MA

New England Medical Center
Inpatient Addition, Boston, MA

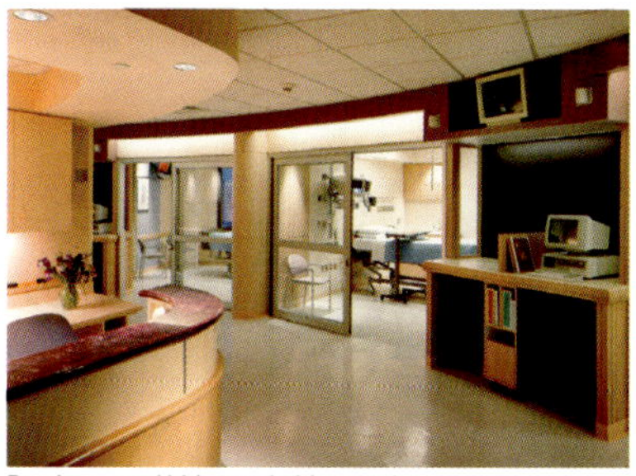
Brigham and Women's Hospital

Lucent Technologies

Massachusetts Water Resources Authority

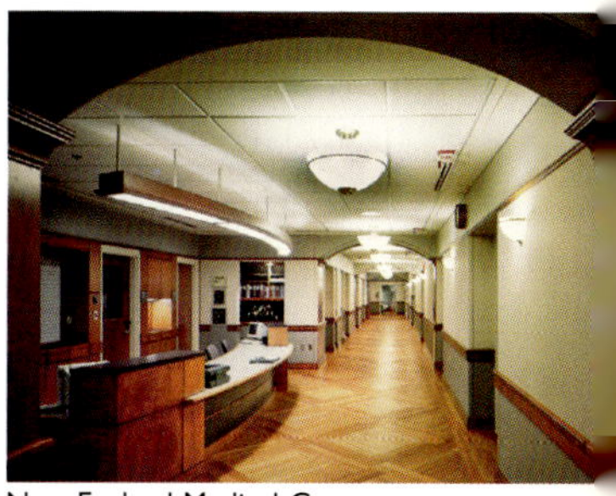
New England Medical Center

1995

Boston Properties
8 Cambridge Center, Cambridge, MA

Forest City Enterprises | Millennium Pharmaceuticals
University Park at MIT, Cambridge, MA

Lehigh Valley Hospital and Health Network
Jaindl Family Pavilion, Lehigh, PA

Lehigh Valley Hospital and Health Network
Main Lobby, Allentown, PA

Lehigh Valley Hospital and Health Network
Master Plan, Allentown, PA

Lehigh Valley Hospital and Health Network
Patient-Centered Inpatient Care Units, Allentown, PA

Magee-Womens Hospital of UPMC
Master Plan, Pittsburgh, PA

Magee-Womens Hospital of UPMC
Womancare Oakland, Pittsburgh, PA

Massachusetts General Hospital
Francis H. Burr Proton Therapy Center, Boston, MA

Massachusetts Port Authority
Bird Island Flats Parking Garage, Boston, MA

MetroHealth Medical Center
Master Plan, Cleveland, OH

New England Medical Center
Patient Care Center, Boston, MA

Planned Parenthood League of Massachusetts
Headquarters, Boston, MA

Suffolk University Law School
David J. Sargent Hall, Boston, MA

University of Chicago Hospitals
The Duchossois Center for Advanced Medicine, Chicago, IL

University of Massachusetts Dartmouth
School for Marine Science and Technology, New Bedford, MA

Lehigh Valley Hospital and Health Network

Planned Parenthood League of Massachusetts

University of Massachusetts Dartmouth

2000

Associates of Cape Cod
Corporate Headquarters, Falmouth, MA

Boston Financial Data Services
Corporate Offices/Customer Service Center, Quincy, MA

Brown University
Biomed Laboratories, Providence, RI

Children's Hospital Boston
Karp Family Research Laboratories, Boston, MA

Clark University
Lasry Center for Bioscience, Worcester, MA

Dartmouth College
Centerra Biology Lab, Lebanon, NH

Dartmouth College
Life Sciences Building Study, Hanover, NH

EMD Serono
North American Headquarters, Hingham, MA

Harvard Business School
Professional Center, Allston, MA

Harvard Law School
Harkness Commons, Cambridge, MA

Harvard Law School
Master Plan, Cambridge, MA

Harvard University John F. Kennedy School of Government
Renovations, Cambridge, MA

Intercontinental Developers
Nine Zero Hotel, Boston, MA

Intercontinental Developers
Winthrop Square, Cambridge, MA

Lyme Properties | BioMed Realty Trust
Center for Life Science Boston, Boston, MA

Lyme Properties
Center for Life Science Houston Study, Houston, TX

Magee-Womens Hospital of UPMC
Neonatal Intensive Care Unit, Pittsburgh, PA

Brown University

Harvard Business School

Harvard University JFK School

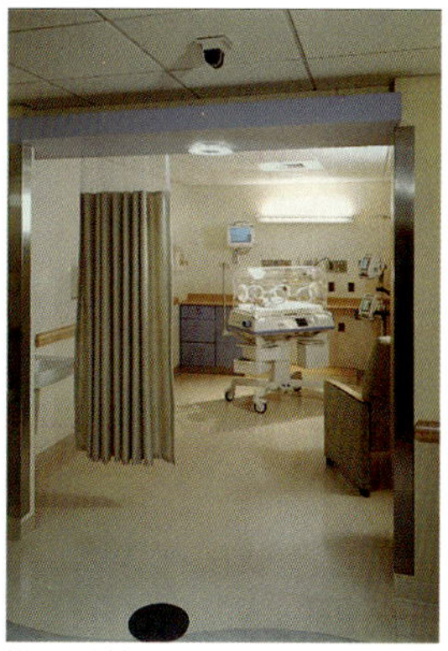
Magee-Womens Hospital of UPMC

Marine Biological Laboratory
C.V. Starr Environmental Sciences Building, Woods Hole, MA

MetroHealth Medical Center
Critical Care Pavilion, Cleveland, OH

MetroHealth Medical Center
Valentine Parking Facility, Cleveland, OH

MIT Real Estate
700 Main Street, Cambridge, MA

Mount Sinai School of Medicine
Medical Education Center Study, New York, NY

Novartis Institute for BioMedical Research
Cambridge, MA

Parametric Technology Corporation | Boston Properties
Corporate Headquarters, Needham, MA

Partners HealthCare
Molecular Biology Research Facilities, Cambridge, MA

Rush University Medical Center
Facility Master Plan, Chicago, IL

Southbridge Associates
Southbridge Hotel & Conference Center, Southbridge, MA

Suffolk University
Mildred F. Sawyer Library, Boston, MA

The Church of Jesus Christ of Latter-Day Saints
Belmont Temple, Belmont, MA

The Cleveland Clinic Foundation
Hillcrest Hospital Bedtower Expansion Study, Cleveland, OH

University of Massachusetts Medical School
Aaron Lazare Medical Research Building, Worcester, MA

University of Pennsylvania School of Medicine | Forest City Enterprises
Center for Translational Research, Philadelphia, PA

Vertex Pharmaceuticals
Corporate Headquarters, Cambridge, MA

Washington University in St. Louis
Earth and Planetary Sciences Building, St. Louis, MO

Washington University in St. Louis
John M. Olin School of Business Expansion Study, St. Louis, MO

Partners HealthCare

Rush University Medical Center

Suffolk University

Vertex Pharmaceuticals

2005

BioMed Realty Trust
Landmark Center at Eastview, Greenburgh, NY

Boston College High School
Campus-Wide Additions and Renovations, Dorchester, MA

Boston Medical Center
Master Plan, Boston, MA

Boston Medical Center
Moakley Building, Boston, MA

Boston Properties
77 CityPoint, Waltham, MA

Brigham and Women's Hospital
Biomedical Imaging Core, Boston, MA

Case Western Reserve University
Medical Sciences Learning Center Programming Study, Cleveland, OH

Children Hospital of Pittsburgh of UPMC
Academic Pediatric Medical Research Building, Pittsburgh, PA

Medical College of Wisconsin and Children's Research Institute
Translational and Biomedical Research Center, Milwaukee, WI

Dana-Farber Cancer Institute
Biostatistics Group, Boston, MA

Davis Marcus Partners
Charles River Plaza, Boston, MA

Fletcher Allen Health Care
Renaissance Project, Burlington, VT

Harvard Graduate School of Education
Master Facility Plan, Cambridge, MA

Harvard University
Biology Research Infrastructure, Cambridge, MA

Harvard University
Laboratory for Integrated Science and Engineering Fit-Out, Cambridge, MA

Harvard University
Northwest Science Building Fit-Out, Cambridge, MA

BioMed Realty Trust

Boston College High School

Medical College of Wisconsin

Immune Disease Institute
Headquarters, Boston, MA

Johnson & Wales University
Center for Culinary Excellence, Providence, RI

Joslin Diabetes Center
Mixed-Use Development Study, Boston, MA

Marine Biological Laboratory
Rowe Laboratory, Woods Hole, MA

Mount Auburn Hospital
Frank Stanton Building, Cambridge, MA

New England Baptist Hospital
Expansion and Renovations, Boston, MA

ProCure Treatment Centers
Proton Therapy Center, Oklahoma City, OK

The Children's Hospital of Philadelphia
South Campus Master Plan, Philadelphia, PA

The Cleveland Clinic Foundation
Master Plan, Cleveland, OH

The Ohio State University Medical Center
Master Site and Facilities Plan, Columbus, OH

The University of Texas M. D. Anderson Cancer Center
Proton Therapy Center, Houston, TX

Thomas Jefferson University and Thomas Jefferson University Hospital
Master Plan, Philadelphia, PA

University of Florida Fredric G. Levin College of Law
Library/Classroom Expansion, Gainesville, FL

University of Florida Proton Therapy Institute
Proton Beam Therapy Center, Jacksonville, FL

University of Massachusetts Medical School
Master Plan, Worcester, MA

University of Massachusetts Medical School | Massachusetts Biologic Laboratories
Drug Discovery and Development R&D and Administration Facility, Mattapan, MA

University of Minnesota Children's Hospital, Fairview
Replacement Hospital, Minneapolis, MN

UNC Hospitals and UNC-Chapel Hill School of Medicine
Master Plan, Chapel Hill, NC

University of Pennsylvania Health System
Roberts Proton Therapy Center, Philadelphia, PA

University of Pennsylvania Health System
West Tower Fit-out, Philadelphia, PA

University of Pennsylvania Health System
Inpatient Tower Replacement Concept Study, Philadelphia, PA

University of Pittsburgh Medical Center
Research Building Study, Pittsburgh, PA

University of Virginia
Translational Medicine Research Building Concept Study, Charlottesville, VA

Washington University in St. Louis School of Medicine
Strategic Facilities Master Plan, St. Louis, MO

Washington University in St. Louis
The William H. and Elizabeth Gray Danforth University Center, St. Louis, MO

Worcester Polytechnic Institute | Newgate Properties
WPI Life Sciences and Bioengineering Center at Gateway Park, Worcester, MA

University of Florida Proton Therapy Institute

University of Massachusetts Medical School

University of Virginia

Worcester Polytechnic Institute | Newgate Properties

2010

Boston College
Campus Green Conceptual Study and Stokes Commons and Lyons Dining Expansion, Newton, MA

Boston Medical Center
Carl J. and Ruth Shapiro Ambulatory Care Center, Boston, MA

Children's Hospital Boston
Children's Brookline Place Medical and Administrative Office Building, Brookline, MA

Cornell University
University Health Services, Ithaca, NY

Duke University Medical Center
Cancer Center, Durham, NC

ProCure Treatment Centers
Proton Therapy Cancer Treatment Center at Central DuPage Hospital, Winfield, IL

Cornell University

Life Sciences Development

Acknowledgments

We would first like to thank our clients, without whom the work celebrated within this monograph would not have been possible. They have provided us with rich and varied challenges, and have been our collaborators and our inspiration throughout. Each client has brought to us a unique opportunity, and we have endeavored to exceed their expectations. It has been our honor and privilege to work with them.

Our projects require the involvement and expertise of the highest-caliber consultants and contractors, and we gratefully acknowledge these key partners, several of whom we have worked with for many years on numerous projects.

We would also like to recognize all current and past staff for their contributions. The success of these projects is a direct result of their talent, hard work, and shared commitment to excellence.

Finally, Tsoi/Kobus & Associates would like to express thanks to the many members of our staff who at one point or another contributed to the production of this, our first monograph. We are especially grateful to Tina Vaz for her extraordinary dedication to this project and for always finding the right words; Katy Tassmer for shepherding the process and minding the flock; Greg Luongo for his contributions in selecting and editing the editorial and graphic content; Matt Cotton for serving as our planning guru; Morgan Madera, Todd Piotrowski, and Chris Goldthwaite for their graphics expertise and coolness under pressure; and David Owens for repeatedly coming through with sketches, often on a moment's notice. We would further like to thank Steve Kliment, Pamela de Oliveira-Smith, and Andrzej Zarzycki as well as Alessina Brooks, Paul Latham, and Andrew Hall of The Images Publishing Group.

Collaborators

Ballinger
Freeman French Freeman
HGA Architects and Engineers
HLM Design
KMD Architects
Nalls Architecture
OWP/P
Solomont Bailis Ventures

Photography Credits

3D WIN	204, 205, 206, 207 (4), 223 (left)
Robert Benson	26, 28–29, 30, 31 (8), 33, (11&13) 34 (15), 35, 76, 78 (4), 80, 81, 82, 83, 88, 89 (11), 106, 107, 108, 109, 116, 117, 118 (5), 142, 144, 145, 146, 147, 148–149, 150 (5), 152, 184, 222 (right)
Christina Caturano	94
Lucy Chen	77, 78 (5), 219 (right), 220 (center right)
Denmarsh Photography	219 (center right)
Mark Flannery	92
Debbie Frank	110, 111, 113, 114, 115,
Harvard Law School	118 (3)
Hedrich Blessing	42, 43, 44, 45, 46, 47, 48, 49, 50, 51, 52, 53, 218 (left), 220 (center)
Henry Ford Museum & Greenfield Village Collection	57 (5&6)
David Hewitt/Anne Garrison	135, 136, 138
Jonathan Hillyer	22, 23, 24, 25, 36, 37, 38, 39, 222 (left)
Anton Grassl	220 (left)
IBA	41 (3)
Warren Jagger	219 (left)
Landslides Aerial Photography	27
David Lamb	221 (left)
Dongik Lee	123 (4), 153, 164, 165, 166, 167, 169, 176, 178, 179, 180, 187, 190, 192, 193, 194, 196, 197, 210, 212, 220 (center left)
LIK Group	199, 203 (6, 7, 8)
Greg Luongo	33 (12)
Bruce Martin	222 (right)
Peter Mauss/Esto	31 (7), 32, 34 (16)
Neoscape	69, 71, 185
Greg Premru	97, 151
Bruce Rogovin	7, 8, 10, 13, 15, 224, 225
Steve Rosenthal	40, 41 (2), 54, 55, 56, 57, 58, 59, 60, 61, 62, 63, 64, 65, 84, 85, 87 (5), 98, 99, 100, 101, 102, 103, 120, 121, 122, 124–125, 126, 128, 129, 134, 135, 137, 138, 139, 154, 155, 156, 157 (4), 158, 159, 160, 161, 216, 217, 218 (right), 219
Rick Scanlan	87 (6), 220 (right)
Seich Peterman Ruffo	95
Jeff Stikeman	186
Sam Sweezy	136, 161
Jeffrey Totaro	18, 19, 20, 21, 68, 130, 131, 132, 133,
Peter Vanderwarker	90, 91, 93
Wilson Architects	143
Ed Wonsek	68, 73 (8), 74–75

Index

Greg Luongo John Lynch Kana Machida Catherine Macor
Ahmed Mahious Julissa Maldonado Tony Mambuca Jennife
Rebecca Martin Liliana Martinez Alexis Masnik Lori M
Jennifer McEntire Diane McKinney Kathy McMahon John
Gregory Meyer Renee Mierzejewski Walter Milano Diana
Judy Mitchell Irene Mitsuhashi Narine Mkrtumian Anne M
Hal Moore Howard Moreno Janice Moreth Christo
Brittany Musselman Marta Nagy Antonio Narciso Laura Nat
Choy Ng **Sapir Ng** Steven Ng Khuthaza Ngodwane-Stu
Julia O'Grady Lisa Oldham Carol Oliva Albert Oliver **Ste**
Jennifer Ossen **David Owens** Bob Pahl Ray Pan Andy P
Aaron Pickering Todd Piotrowski Serge Plishevsky Gloria
Jenny Putnam Laura Pyper Michael Quinlan Amy Raddan
Jennifer Rayburn Robert Raymond Rita Reamer **Mark**
Ana Restrepo Heidi Richards Jeff Rizzo Scott Roaf Craig
Ann Saldi Charles Samson Paul San Gemino Jose Luis
Pat Schultz Brenda Senecal Karen Shaknites Lisa Shaw
James Skypeck David Smith Jennifer Smith Beth Ann Sm
Matt Spicer Erica Steenstra Scott Steffes Laura Stevens D
Chris Sweet Robert Sweet **Jack Synnott** Rebecca Szew
Howard Thompson Courtney Thornton Kathleen Thorpe
Ted Touloukian Brandon Townsend Barbara Trissel Rob Tru
Allan Vanderley Frank Vardaxis Sondae Varga Arturo Vas
Dennis Vigliotte **John Vinton** Pia Von Allmen Amita Wa
Chenling Wang Emily Wang Catherine Warsen Ellen
Ellen Whittemore Rick Wilcox Ken Williams Andrew
Ethan Yungerman Andrzej Zarzycki Susana Zelter Matthe